THE
NEW
CLASS WAR

THE
NEW
CLASS WAR

Saving Democracy from the
Managerial Elite

MICHAEL LIND

PORTFOLIO / PENGUIN

PORTFOLIO / PENGUIN
An imprint of Penguin Random House LLC
penguinrandomhouse.com

Copyright © 2020 by Michael Lind
Penguin supports copyright. Copyright fuels creativity, encourages
diverse voices, promotes free speech, and creates a vibrant culture. Thank you
for buying an authorized edition of this book and for complying with copyright
laws by not reproducing, scanning, or distributing any part of it in any form
without permission. You are supporting writers and allowing Penguin
to continue to publish books for every reader.

Most Portfolio books are available at a discount when purchased in
quantity for sales promotions or corporate use. Special editions, which include
personalized covers, excerpts, and corporate imprints, can be created when
purchased in large quantities. For more information, please call (212) 572-2232 or
e-mail specialmarkets@penguinrandomhouse.com. Your local bookstore can also
assist with discounted bulk purchases using the Penguin Random House
corporate Business-to-Business program. For assistance in locating a
participating retailer, e-mail B2B@penguinrandomhouse.com.

ISBN: 9780593083697 (hardcover)
ISBN: 9780593083703 (ebook)

Printed in the United States of America
1   3   5   7   9   10   8   6   4   2

BOOK DESIGN BY TANYA MAIBORODA

Contents

The problem of classes is this: Class conflict is essential if freedom is to be preserved, because it is the only barrier against class domination; yet class conflict, pursued to excess, may well destroy the underlying fabric of common principle which sustains free society.

—ARTHUR M. SCHLESINGER JR.,
The Vital Center: The Politics of Freedom (1949)

No theory, no promises, no morality, no amount of good will, no religion will restrain power. . . . Only power restrains power.

—JAMES BURNHAM,
The Machiavellians: Defenders of Freedom (1943)

Introduction

O N THE NIGHT OF July 14, 1789, legend has it, news of the fall of the Bastille was brought by a duke to the king of France, Louis XVI. "Then it's a revolt?" the king asked. The duke replied: "No, sire, it's a revolution."

On June 23, 2016, a majority of British voters passed the Brexit referendum requiring the United Kingdom to leave the European Union. A few months after that political earthquake, on November 8, 2016, came an even more shocking event: the election of Donald Trump as president of the United States.

Since then, throughout Europe, centrist parties have lost voters to outsider parties and politicians—sometimes on the left but more often on the populist and nationalist right. In the summer of 2018, a coalition of the right-wing populist League and the antiestablishment Five Star Movement came to power in Italy. In Germany, the center-left Social Democrats imploded, losing voters to insurgent movements on the right and left. Nations that were said to be immune to nationalist populism, like Sweden, Germany, and Spain, have seen insurgent populist parties enter their parliaments.

Under Emmanuel Macron, a former civil servant and investment banker who defeated the national populist candidate Marine Le Pen in 2017, France at first seemed immune to upheaval. "Emmanuel Macron's victory in the French presidential election clearly demonstrates that the populist dominos in advanced economies outside the Anglo-Saxon world were not even close to falling," Jacob Funk Kirkegaard, a senior fellow at the Peterson Institute for International Economics (PIIE), a free market think tank in Washington, DC, declared in May 2017, in an essay entitled "Macron's Victory Signals Reform in France and a Stronger Europe."[1] Nearly a year later, in April 2018, Will Marshall of the Progressive Policy Institute, an architect of the "New Democrat" movement associated with the Clintons, published an essay in *Politico* arguing that the French president proved that promarket neoliberal centrists could defeat the forces of populism and nationalism: "How Emmanuel Macron Became the New Leader of the Free World."[2]

Then, beginning in November 2018, protests that were initially directed against the impact of an increase in fuel prices on suburban, small-town, and rural French working-class citizens escalated into months of violent clashes among police and protesters that filled central Paris with tear gas and burning cars and ignited protests across France.

"Then it's a revolt?"

"No, sire, it's a revolution."

Indeed it is. Europe and North America are experiencing the greatest revolutionary wave of political protest since the 1960s or perhaps the 1930s.[3] Except in France, the transatlantic revolution to date has remained nonviolent. But it is a revolution nonetheless.

To QUOTE THE saying of the radicals of the 1960s: *the issue is not the issue.* If the immediate issues that animate mostly native working-class populism in particular countries—immigration and trade for Trump, immigration and sovereignty for Brexiteers, high levels of Muslim immigration for German and Scandinavian populists, fuel prices and other domestic policies whose costs fall chiefly on the peripheral working class, in the case of the French yellow vest protestors—are not *the* issue, then what *is* the issue?

The issue is power. Social power exists in three realms—government, the economy, and the culture. Each of these three realms of social power is the site of class conflict—sometimes intense and sometimes contained by interclass compromises. All three realms of Western society today are fronts in the new class war.

The first class war in the West began a century and a half ago, in the early stages of industrialization, when the premodern agrarian social structure was shattered by the emergence of the two major modern social classes: industrial or service workers on the one hand and, on the other, bourgeois capitalists, later joined by university-credentialed managers and professionals. Reforms were partial and limited, until the imperative of mobilizing entire national populations for war made ending class conflict a necessity.

During and after World War II, the United States and its Western European allies, often on the basis of wartime precedents, adopted versions of what I describe in this book as democratic pluralism. In the America of Truman and Eisenhower, the Germany of Adenauer, the Britain of Churchill, and other Western democracies, power brokers who answered to working-class and rural constituencies—grassroots party politicians, trade union and farm association leaders, and church leaders—bargained with national elites in the three realms of government, the economy, and the culture, respectively. In the era of democratic pluralism, the societies of the North Atlantic enjoyed mass prosperity and reduced inequality.

Between the 1960s and the present, as declining fear of great-power conflict gradually reduced the incentives of Western elites to make concessions to Western working classes, the postwar system has been dismantled in a revolution from above that has promoted the material interests and intangible values of the college-educated minority of managers and professionals, who have succeeded old-fashioned bourgeois capitalists as the dominant elite.

What has replaced democratic pluralism can be described as technocratic neoliberalism. In the realm of the economy, corporations have promoted deunionization and labor market deregulation to the detriment of workers. Firms have also embraced global labor arbitrage, in the form of offshoring production to poor workers abroad or employing immigrant workers, to weaken unions and escape the constraints of national labor regulations.

Meanwhile, in the realm of politics and government, parties that were national federations of local, mass-membership organizations have given way to parties controlled by donors and media consultants. At the same time, many of the powers of democratic national legislatures have been usurped by, or delegated to, executive agencies, courts, or transnational bodies over which college-educated professionals have far more influence than the working-class majority, whether native- or foreign-born.

Finally, in the realm of culture, including media and education, local religious and civic watchdogs have lost power, often as a result of activism by judges born into the social elite who share their libertarian economic and social views with their university-educated peers.

The technocratic neoliberal revolution from above, carried out in one Western nation after another by members of the ever more aggressive and powerful managerial elite, has provoked a populist backlash from below by the defensive and disempowered native working class, many of whom are nonwhite (a substantial minority of black and ethnic British voters supported Brexit, and in the US an estimated 29 percent of Latinos voted in 2016 for Trump).[4] Large numbers of alienated working-class voters, realizing that the political systems of their nations are rigged and that mainstream parties will continue to ignore their interests and values, have found sometimes unlikely champions in demagogic populists like Donald Trump, Nigel Farage, Boris Johnson, Marine Le Pen, and Matteo Salvini.

For all their differences, these populist demagogues have launched similar counterattacks on dominant neoliberal establishments in all three realms of social power. In the realm of the economy, populists favor national restrictions on trade and immigration to shield workers from competing with imports and immigrants. In the realm of politics, populists denounce neoliberal parties and factions as corrupt and elitist. And in the realm of culture, populists denounce elite-promulgated multiculturalism and globalism, while deliberately flouting the norms of the "politically correct" etiquette that marks membership in the university-educated managerial elite.

Will populists in Europe and North America succeed in overthrowing and replacing technocratic neoliberalism? Almost certainly not. Populist voters are a substantial and enduring part of Western electorates, but they are only one constituency in pluralistic societies with increasingly fragmented political systems.

Moreover, populist demagogues tend to be charlatans. They are often corrupt. Many are racist or ethnocentric, though these traits are exaggerated by establishment critics who compare them to Mussolini and Hitler. While demagogic populists can win occasional isolated victories for their voters, history suggests that populist movements are likely to fail when confronting well-entrenched ruling classes whose members enjoy near monopolies of expertise, wealth, and cultural influence.

In response to populist rebellions from below, the managerial elites of various Western countries may turn to outright repression of the working class by restricting access to political activity and the media by all dissenters, not populists alone. As an alternative, the managerial ruling classes may try to co-opt populist rebels by making minor concessions on immigration, trade, or domestic policy.

But sharing wealth through redistribution and symbolic gestures of respect are unlikely to end the new class war, if the small managerial overclass is not willing to share genuine power with the working-class majority. Achieving a genuine class peace in the democracies of the West will require uniting and empowering both native and immigrant workers while restoring genuine decision-making power to the non-university-educated majority in all three realms of social power—the economy, politics, and culture.

Demagogic populism is a symptom. Technocratic neoliberalism is the disease. Democratic pluralism is the cure.

THE
NEW
CLASS WAR

CHAPTER ONE

The New Class War

T HE COLD WAR has been followed by the class war. A transatlantic class war has broken out simultaneously in many Western countries between elites based in the corporate, financial, government, media, and educational sectors and disproportionately native working-class populists. The old spectrum of left and right has given way to a new dichotomy in politics among insiders and outsiders.*

None of the dominant political ideologies of the West can explain the new class war, because all of them pretend that enduring, self-perpetuating social classes no longer exist in the West.

Technocratic neoliberalism—the hegemonic ideology of the transatlantic elite—pretends that inherited class status has virtually disappeared in societies that are purely meritocratic, with the exception of barriers to individual upward

---

* The democracies of North America and Western Europe are similar enough to justify generalizations about them. Political and social developments in Eastern Europe, East Asia, and other parts of the world are beyond the scope of this book.

mobility that still exist because of racism and misogyny. Unable to acknowledge the existence of social class, much less to discuss conflicts among classes, neoliberals tend to attribute populism to bigotry or frustration on the part of maladjusted individuals or a resurgence of 1930s fascism or the sinister machinations of Russian president Vladimir Putin's nationalist regime.

Like neoliberalism, mainstream conservatism assumes that hereditary classes no longer exist in the West. Along with neoliberals and libertarians, establishment conservatives claim that the economic elite is not a semihereditary class but rather an ever-changing, kaleidoscopic aggregate of talented and hardworking individuals. According to libertarian conservative ideology, the short-term interests of employers are always identical with those of workers and society as a whole. In conventional conservative thought, meritocratic capitalism is threatened from within by an anticapitalist "new class" consisting of progressive intellectuals—professors, journalists, and nonprofit activists.

For its part, Marxism takes classes and class conflict seriously. But orthodox Marxism, with its secularized providential theory of history and its view of industrial workers as the cosmopolitan agents of global revolution, has always been absurd.

A body of thought does exist that can explain the current upheavals in the West and the world. It is James Burnham's theory of the managerial revolution, supplemented by the economic sociology of John Kenneth Galbraith. Burnham's thought has recently enjoyed a revival among thinkers of the American center-right.[1] Unfortunately, Galbraith's sociology, along with his economics, remains out of fashion.[2]

James Burnham was a leader in the international Trotskyist movement in the 1930s before he became a zealous anticommunist and helped to found the post–World War II American conservative movement. Burnham was influenced by the argument of Adolf Berle and Gardiner Means in *The Modern Corporation and Private Property* (1932), which documented the separation of ownership and control in large-scale modern enterprises, and possibly by Bruno Rizzi's *Bureaucratization of the World* (1939).[3] In his worldwide bestseller *The Managerial Revolution* (1941), Burnham argued that in the era of large-scale capitalism and the bureaucratic state, the older bourgeoisie was being replaced by a new managerial class:

> What is occurring in this transition is a drive for social domination, for power and privilege, for the position of ruling class, by the social group or class of the *managers*. . . . At the conclusion of the transition period the managers will, in fact, have achieved social dominance, will be the ruling class in society. This drive, moreover, is world-wide in extent, already well advanced in all nations, though at different levels of development in different nations.[4]

In his essay "Second Thoughts on James Burnham" (1946), George Orwell provided a succinct summary of Burnham's thesis:

> Capitalism is disappearing, but Socialism is not replacing it. What is now arising is a new kind of planned, centralized society which will be neither capitalist nor,

in any accepted sense of the word, democratic. The rulers of this new society will be the people who effectively control the means of production: that is, business executives, technicians, bureaucrats and soldiers, lumped together by Burnham, under the name of "managers." These people will eliminate the old capitalist class, crush the working class, and so organize society that all power and economic privilege remain in their own hands. Private property rights will be abolished, but common ownership will not be established. The new "managerial" societies will not consist of a patchwork of small, independent states, but of great super-states grouped round the main industrial centres in Europe, Asia, and America. These super-states will fight among themselves for possession of the remaining uncaptured portions of the earth, but will probably be unable to conquer one another completely. Internally, each society will be hierarchical, with an aristocracy of talent at the top and a mass of semi-slaves at the bottom.[5]

Following the abandonment of communism, the global norm in both developed and developing countries, democratic and authoritarian alike, has been some version of the mixed economy dominated by bureaucratic corporations, bureaucratic government, and bureaucratic nonprofits, which are staffed by university-credentialed national elites who circulate among the three sectors. What Orwell called Burnham's "great super-states grouped round the main industrial centres in Europe, Asia, and America" exist today under the names of NATO and NAFTA, the EU, Russia's Eurasian Economic Union (EAEU), and the informal sphere of influence coalescing around China.

While private property rights have not been abolished, even in so-called capitalist countries they have been diluted and redefined beyond recognition. Vast numbers of temporary holders of corporate shares that are frequently bought and resold by intermediaries like mutual funds are said to "own" corporations. Ordinary people with loan repayment or installment plans who in effect are renting houses, cars, and phones from banks or corporations likewise are owners in name only.

Burnham's theory of the managerial revolution is similar to the economic sociology of the American economist John Kenneth Galbraith. In their politics, the conservative Burnham and the liberal Galbraith could hardly have been more different from each other, despite their shared friendship with the influential conservative editor and journalist William F. Buckley Jr. Yet both believed that a new ruling elite had displaced the old bourgeoisie and aristocracy. In *The New Industrial State* (1967), Galbraith called the new elite the "technostructure." In his memoir *A Life in Our Times* (1981), Galbraith wrote: "James Burnham, partly because he was a stalwart right-winger well out of the political mainstream and partly because he was not a certified academician, never got full credit for his contribution. In early editions of *The New Industrial State* I was among those in default."[6]

While Burnham and Galbraith included engineers and

scientists in the new elite, they were not describing a technocracy like the utopian "soviet of technicians" hoped for by the maverick economist Thorstein Veblen.[7] The most important managers are private and public bureaucrats who run large national and global corporations, government agencies, and nonprofit organizations. They exercise disproportionate influence in politics and society by virtue of their institutional positions in large, powerful bureaucracies. Some are independently wealthy, but most are salaried employees or fee-earning professionals. Most of today's billionaires were born into this university-educated, credentialed, bureaucratic upper middle class, and their heirs tend to disappear back into it in a generation or two. Premodern titled aristocrats who survive in the contemporary West are anachronisms who, for the most part, avoid ridicule by disguising themselves as hardworking professionals and managers.

IN MY BOOK *The Next American Nation* (1995), I used the term "overclass" to describe this group of college-educated managers and professionals.

How big is the overclass? It's difficult to measure, but operating on Mark Bovens and Anchrit Wille's theory that Western democracies are "diploma democracies"—"ruled by the citizens with the highest degrees"—we can count higher education as a market of membership in the overclass.[8]

In both Europe and the US, only about three out of ten citizens have college degrees, and that a third of the population provides almost all government, business, media, and nonprofit personnel. Even fewer citizens have the professional or graduate degrees that more accurately correspond with membership in the college-educated managerial overclass—no more than 10 or 15 percent of the population in a typical Western nation, a small minority, though considerably larger than the much-discussed "1 percent." This credentialed overclass owns roughly half the wealth in the United States, with the rest divided between the superrich and the bottom 90 percent.[9]

Are the managers and professionals an inbred, self-perpetuating, hereditary class as well as an educational elite? In a purely meritocratic society, the ranks of university-educated managers and professionals might be refilled completely by upwardly mobile individuals in each generation. In the United States, however, American college students tend to have one or more college-educated parents. In other Western democracies as well, membership in the university-educated managerial class is also partly hereditary, though partly open to talent from below.[10]

In the United States and Europe, intergenerational mobility, measured crudely by correlation between the earnings of fathers and sons, is strikingly low. According to Julia B. Isaacs of the Brookings Institution, roughly half of the "parental earnings advantage" is inherited by sons: "If trends hold, it would take an average of six generations for family economic advantage to disappear in the United States and the United Kingdom." In Canada, Norway, Finland, and Denmark, social mobility is somewhat higher, such that "it would take three, not six, generations, to essentially cancel out the effects of being born into a wealthy family."[11] If only

America were more like social democratic Europe, it would take only three generations to make a gentleman.

The persistence of class in Britain is even more striking. Gregory Clark and Neil Cummins have demonstrated that Britons with Norman French surnames like Darcy, Mandeville, Percy, and Montgomery have been at the top of the British social order for twenty-seven generations since the Norman conquest in 1066, while families with Anglo-Saxon names like Sidwell, Tonbridge, and Goodhill still tend to be poorer and less educated.[12]

It may be true that college degrees are tickets out of poverty, but most of the tickets are passed out at birth to children in a small number of families with a lot of money. In the United States, students with math scores in the bottom half who come from families with the highest socioeconomic status are more likely to finish a college degree than students from families with the lowest socioeconomic status who have math scores in the top half of the range.[13] In a true meritocracy, the mediocre children of college-educated parents would constantly be tumbling down into the non-college-educated working class, replaced by smarter, upwardly mobile scions of the working class. But overclass families will do anything they can to make sure that their offspring remain in the university-credentialed elite into which they were born, including, in the United States, bribing university admissions officials and reference letter writers.

The Industrial Revolution did not replace class systems in the West with classless, meritocratic societies. It replaced the old, mostly hereditary class system consisting of landlords and peasants with a new, mostly hereditary class system consisting of managers and proles, in which degrees are the new titles of nobility and diplomas the new coats of arms.

I S THE MANAGERIAL OVERCLASS global or national? The new class war, in its international dimension, is not a classic Marxist struggle of postnational capitalists against a global working class. Nor is it the work of rootless "globalists" of the kind sometimes denounced by populists. Today's Western managerial elites often pretend to be "citizens of the world," and signal their virtue by disdaining the democratic nation-state as parochial or anachronistic. But most are deeply rooted in their home countries.

While many supply chains are now regional or global, the headquarters of the global economy are not only in the triad of North America–Europe–Northeast Asia but also dispropor-tionately in the US, Japan, Germany, and the UK. Of the top ten multinationals by foreign assets in 2016, three were based in the US (Chevron, General Electric, ExxonMobil), two in the UK (the oil companies Royal Dutch Shell and BP), two in Japan (Toyota, SoftBank), and one apiece in Germany (Volks-wagen), France (Total), and Belgium (Anheuser-Busch In-Bev).[14] Even when they establish transplant operations in the territories of other developed nations, leading multinational firms, like Toyota, Daimler, and Ford, tend to retain their na-tional identity at the leadership level.

Nor has a transnational managerial elite replaced national managerial elites. In the United States, foreign-born CEOs in 2015 accounted for only seventy-three, or 14.6 percent, of Fortune 500 CEOs. As of 2014, international revenue made up 37 percent of total revenue for S&P 500 firms, but the share of directors who were foreign nationals was only 7.2 percent.[15]

The new class war is not a global class war. It consists of struggles in particular Western nations among local over-classes and local working classes, struggles that happen to be taking place in many nations at the same time.

O N BOTH SIDES of the Atlantic, the political divide between the educated overclass and the rest of the country is stark. In the 2016 US presidential election, among counties with a population of fifty thousand or more, Hillary Clinton won forty-eight of the fifty counties that had the highest percentage of voters with at least a four-year bachelor's degree. Support for her presidential bid "collapsed" (to use the pollster Nate Silver's term) in the fifty counties with the lowest educational levels. Political differences correlated with education can be found among racial and ethnic minority populations as well.[16]

The same pattern is evident in Europe. In Britain, for example, the chief trait predicting support for the Leave side in the Brexit referendum in 2016 was lower educational qualifications—a trait that was more important than others, including race and ethnicity.[17] Because the possession of a diploma tends to indicate birth into the economic elite, these figures manifest conflict among largely hereditary social classes, not a clash between knowledge and ignorance or intelligence and stupidity.

If a united working class voted against the overclass, the latter would lose every election. But national working classes

have always been divided in politics by various cleavages—
religious, regional, racial, ethnic, and ideological—to the
benefit of outnumbered managerial elites. The most important cleavage dividing the working classes in today's North
Atlantic democracies is rivalry for jobs, public services, and
status among old-stock natives and recent immigrants and
their descendants. To understand this rift within the working class, we must add to James Burnham's analysis of managerial rule the split labor market theory first proposed by
sociologist Edna Bonacich in 1972.[18]

According to Bonacich, a split labor market occurs when
there are "at least two groups of workers whose price of labor differs for the same work, or would differ if they did the
same work." In the case of some regional or ethnic groups:
"Crushing poverty may drive them to sell their labor relatively cheaply." In this situation, employers will prefer to
hire members of the group willing to work for lower wages.
In response, higher-paid workers will attempt to maintain
their standard of wages by preventing employers from doing
so, by excluding the rival group and confining it to certain occupations in a segregated, caste-like system, or by leveling the
playing field so that there are no group-based wage differen-
tials. According to the historian Gavin Wright, by eliminat-
ing the split labor market that existed under segregation, the
civil rights revolution contributed to economic growth and
more widely shared prosperity in the American South in the
final decades of the twentieth century.[19]

Split labor market theory is a great improvement on
the simpleminded explanation of the opposition of native

workers to immigrant rivals or workers competing with them abroad as the result of preexisting individual prejudice. Bonacich complained that "both Marxist and non-Marxist writers assume that racial and cultural differences in themselves prompt the development of ethnic competition. This theory challenges that assumption, suggesting that economic processes are more fundamental."

The description of the new class war here is simplified for clarity. There are many fine gradations and categories that must be left out of a book like this. The university-credentialed overclass contains moderately paid schoolteachers and store managers as well as wealthy corporate lawyers and billionaire entrepreneurs. Workers who did not go to college include prosperous construction contractors as well as high school dropouts who work as janitors or laborers employed by moving companies.

Even with these qualifications, the pattern of politics in today's Western democracies is best described as a struggle with three sides—the overclass and two segments of a divided working class. Working-class immigrants and some native minority group members whose personal conditions are improving compete with many members of the native working class, mostly but not exclusively white, who find their economic status, political power, and cultural dignity under threat from below as well as from above. The only winners are a third group: the mostly native, mostly white overclass elites who benefit from the division of the working class.

"All politics is local," as the old American saying has it. In modern Western democracies, the division of the national territory into federal subunits and voting districts means that class conflict is manifested by geographic differences in partisanship and worldview. In the next chapter I will explore the geographic battlegrounds of contemporary politics on both sides of the Atlantic—hubs and heartlands.

CHAPTER TWO

Hubs and Heartlands: The Battlegrounds of the New Class War

O N A MAP OF the United States color-coded by party, big cities and university towns and a few regions with large immigrant and racial minority populations are a chain of Democratic islands in a Republican ocean. Similar patterns appear on maps of voting for Brexit in the UK and elections in continental Europe.

Looking at these maps, it is easy to see why scholars and journalists refer to the "urban-rural divide." But this is misleading. Farm owners and farmworkers make up only a tiny sliver of the population in the typical Western democracy. Most voters in Europe and North America today live in broadly defined metro areas or small communities on their periphery. In the case of partisanship, the most important border is not between city and countryside, but between expensive, high-density urban business districts and inner suburbs on the one hand and, on the other, low-density suburbs and exurbs.

Rather than use the terms "city" and "countryside," we

can describe the high-density areas as "hubs" and the low-density areas around and between the hubs as "heartlands."

The hubs and heartlands are distinguished not only by population density but also by different economic sectors. In the hubs, home to most of the managerial overclass, we see two primary sectors: high-end business and professional services, and luxury services. In the heartlands, we find two other sectors: goods production and what can be described as "mass services."[1]

The high-end business and professional services concentrated in the hubs, which Saskia Sassen has called "global cities," such as New York and London, include software, finance, insurance, accounting, marketing, advertising, consulting, and others whose clients are often corporations, including global corporations managing supply chains in many countries.[2] No matter where they are born, professionals and managers often move to pursue their careers in major hub cities that specialize in particular producer services—software in San Francisco and the Bay Area, finance in New York and London and Frankfurt.

Much of the discretionary income of elite managers and professionals in the hub cities is spent on luxury services. In Europe and North America, these amenities are provided by the sectors that the economist David Autor calls "wealth work," a category with formal job titles that include Gift Wrapper, Fingernail Former, Mystery Shopper, and Barista.[3] The combination of low wages and high living costs for many workers in hubs like New York, London, and Paris make these occupations unattractive to many native workers of all races, as well as more prosperous immigrants, who often move to suburbs or exurbs as soon as they can afford to escape. Urban service jobs are filled disproportionately by recent immigrants, for whom miserable pay and crowded living conditions in the hubs are preferable to the limited opportunities in the countries they left behind.

The social liberalism of these high-end service meccas cannot disguise their extreme inequality. The gap between richest and poorest in New York City is comparable to that of Swaziland; Los Angeles and Chicago are slightly more egalitarian, comparable to the Dominican Republic and El Salvador.[4]

Meanwhile, in the vast areas of low-density, low-rise residential and commercial zones around and among the hierarchical hubs, a radically different society has evolved. In the national heartlands, apart from expensive rural resort areas, there are fewer rich households and therefore fewer working poor employed by the rich as servants and luxury service providers.

In the US and Europe, the population of the heartlands is much more likely to be native-born and white. But the heartlands are becoming more racially and ethnically diverse, making the familiar equation of "urban" and "nonwhite" anachronistic. For example, most African Americans and Latinos in the US are neither poor nor urban but belong along with most white Americans to the suburban and exurban working class.[5] Over time, the share of the heartland population that is nonwhite or mixed race is growing, as both nonwhite immigrants and native minority-group members are driven by rising real estate costs out of hub cities that have grown whiter and richer thanks to gentrification. In the United States, immigrants from Latin America are assimilating to mainstream language and culture and marrying outside of their group at a rate similar to that of European immigrants in the past.[6] It is a mistake, therefore, to assume that the hub city ethnic diasporas of today will endure rather than wither away in time as did America's "Little Italys" and "Little Bohemias."

In the heartlands are found almost all of the goods-producing industries that have not been offshored to other countries—factories, farms, mines, and oil and gas wells. In addition to being the realm of goods production, the heartland is the land of mass services. In the somewhat idealized era of mid-twentieth-century industrial Fordism, the workers in mass-production industries earned enough to buy the products they made, such as cars, radios, and television sets. In the twenty-first century, the workers in mass-provision service industries—waiters at inexpensive chain restaurants with working-class clienteles at exurban highway intersections, for example, unlike waiters at prestigious downtown restaurants—often can afford to purchase the services they provide, in a kind of service-sector Fordism.

In short, the hub-heartland divide that is reshaping politics on both sides of the Atlantic is the geographic manifestation of a class divide. Partisan geographic differences tend to be proxies for class conflicts, with the interests of hub city overclasses and heartland working classes colliding when it comes to environmental policies, trade, immigration, and values.

O F ALL OF the self-serving myths that are found in metropolitan overclass propaganda, the most absurd is the idea that the hubs are more "productive" than the heartlands.

This makes sense only if productivity is equated with income. By this standard, if all the billionaires in the United States moved to Jackson Hole, Wyoming, the luxury resort community would become the most "productive" area in the US overnight.

In reality, affluent investors, managers, and professionals in global hubs like New York, San Francisco, and London are paid for the services or capital they provide to major industries or firms, most of which have physical production or transportation facilities elsewhere. The fortunes of many San Francisco tech executives depend on legions of underpaid factory workers in China and other countries, on energy-hungry server farms located in remote rural areas, and on massive communications and transportation infrastructures stretching over vast distances among cities and nations and maintained by blue-collar workers.

Michael Cembalest of J.P. Morgan Asset Management writes that without US heartland regions, "cities would not be able to grow as they have, and/or the US would be highly reliant on geopolitically insecure and costlier imports of food and energy, and be exposed to volatile weather, environmental and exchange rate conditions out of its control." As a tongue-in-cheek thought experiment, Cembalest allocated the 538 votes in the electoral college that elects the US president to American states on the basis of two equally weighted factors, their populations and their food and energy production: "Texas, the Midwest and the Rockies gain electors, while East Coast states and Michigan lose them."[7] Without any irony William Jennings Bryan, the leading agrarian populist of the late nineteenth and early twentieth centuries, would have approved, having declared: "The great cities rest upon our broad and fertile prairies. Burn down your cities and leave our farms, and your cities will spring up again as if by magic; but destroy our farms, and grass will grow in the streets of every city in the country."[8]

Most of the physical production that remains in Western nations, like manufacturing, agriculture, and mining, including fossil fuel extraction, along with infrastructure construction and upkeep, occur far from the fashionable downtowns and affluent, inner-ring suburbs where most of the managerial overclass lives and works. Overclass elites in urban hubs therefore can favor stringent environmental regulations at little cost to themselves. Heartland communities are more likely to be sensitive to the costs of environmental policies than hub city managers and professionals. What is more, the property-owning, working-class majorities of the heartlands are also likely to be more sensitive to environmental restrictions on what property owners can do with their property than the denizens of the hubs, where not only the working poor and the working class but also many professionals must rent because they cannot afford to own homes. And most working-class individuals in low-density regions rely on their personal cars or trucks for commuting, shopping, and recreation.

The French yellow vest riots of the winter of 2018–19 illustrated the intersecting fault lines of class and place in environmental policy. Although France is responsible for only a negligible amount of global greenhouse gas emissions, in order to advertise France's moral leadership in combating global warming, President Macron's government raised taxes on diesel-fueled cars and trucks. The costs of this exercise in

virtue signaling fell disproportionately on working-class and
rural citizens, dependent on their automobiles and trucks.
Their spontaneous protests escalated into months of violence
in Paris and other French cities, forcing Macron's government
to abandon the policy.[9] Subsequently in 2019 the conservative party in Australia, based in low-density working-class
areas, came from behind and defeated a progressive party
that pushed environmental regulations that threatened jobs
and low living costs in the periphery.[10]

L IKE DEBATES ABOUT the environment, debates about
trade are battlefields in the class war. The overclass population living in hubs continues to tout the benefits of trade
liberalization among high-wage and low-wage countries,
including slightly lower prices for consumers for imports
from low-wage nations, but much of the Western working
class is no longer listening. As manufacturing jobs disappear
overseas, disproportionately affecting the livelihoods of the
working class in the heartland, more and more disaffected
Americans look to leaders who promise to change the trade
balance, economic orthodoxy be damned. In 2016, according to the economists David Autor, David Dorn, Gordon
Hanson, and Kaveh Majlesi, voters in US regions exposed to
Chinese import competition were more likely than others
to support the outsider candidacies of Donald Trump and
Bernie Sanders: "Trade-exposed [congressional] districts with
an initial majority white population or initially in Republican hands became substantially more likely to elect a conservative Republican, while trade-exposed districts with an

initial majority-minority population or initially in Democratic hands also became more likely to elect a liberal Democrat. In presidential elections, counties with greater trade exposure shifted towards the Republican candidate."[11]

THE MOST IMPORTANT of the many divisions between the overclass in the hubs and the native working-class voters in the heartland is the clash over immigration policy. Like trade policy in today's era of transnational production, immigration policy is essentially labor policy. Immigration has always been a flash point in the class war between employers and workers.

Members of the mostly white overclass elite in the US often personally benefit from lax enforcement of immigration laws. The Pew Research Center reports that in the US, immigrants make up nearly half of all household servants, who are employed by a relatively small number of affluent households.[12] As Lynn Stuart Parramore writes for the left-leaning *AlterNet*, "In the US, nearly half of maids and housekeepers are not native-born, with Latin Americans dominating. (A big chunk of the wealthy is happy to support mass immigration of cheap labor so that these workers can continue to be underpaid.)"[13]

The adoption by many US hub cities of seemingly idealistic "sanctuary city" laws, which forbid local law enforcement officers from collaborating with federal officials in identifying and deporting illegal immigrants, saves money for managers and professionals by maintaining their access to local pools of low-wage, untaxed, unregulated, off-the-books nannies, as well as other luxury service labor that allows college-educated professionals to maintain their privileged lifestyles. By one estimate, 90 percent of nannies in New York City are paid off the books by employers who ignore employment rules and tax laws.[14]

High levels of immigration, both legal and illegal, also maintain the populations and economies and real estate prices of overclass-dominated hubs. For decades, there has been a net outflow of US citizens moving out of unaffordable big cities like New York, San Francisco, and Los Angeles and their counterparts in Europe. If international migration had not compensated for the exodus of natives from the 1970s onward, New York City would have lost population and its property tax base would have shrunk by $500 billion over thirty years.[15]

Absent perpetual repopulation from abroad, cities like New York, San Francisco, London, and Paris might go into demographic and economic death spirals. Luxury industries, including tourist businesses, might cost more in a tight labor market, while urban real estate prices might tumble, with disastrous consequences for the wealth of local elites. At the same time, the flight of natives from the hubs might accelerate further if two-earner professional couples had to pay higher wages to their servants.

In contrast, curtailing low-wage immigration from abroad would not harm and in some cases might help the working classes employed by the production industries and the mass-service industries of the national heartlands in America and Europe. Few of them can afford foreign-born nannies, maids, and gardeners. And if tighter labor markets allow waiters at suburban chain restaurants to earn more, they can also spend more, not only on mass-provided services but also on mass-produced goods like those at the discount furniture outlet at the highway intersection. Tighter labor markets would make it easier for exploited urban immigrants to demand higher wages from miserly employers as well.

WORKING-CLASS IMMIGRANTS COMPETE with native workers for more than just wages. In modern Western welfare states, lower-paid workers may compete with better-paid workers for limited public resources such as schools, hospitals, welfare services, or, in some countries, public housing. Even in the absence of direct occupational rivalry, this competition for public goods among ethnically divided sections of the working class can provoke resentment.

Within democratic countries, natives and immigrants also compete for status and recognition of their cultures. Under the double standard of what the political scientist Eric Kaufmann calls "asymmetrical multiculturalism," political and media establishments in Europe and the US, atoning for the white supremacist attitudes of earlier generations, praise immigrants and native minorities and celebrate their cultural traditions. In itself, this is commendable progress. Unfortunately, under the logic of asymmetrical multiculturalism, appreciation of minority and immigrant traditions is often coupled with elite contempt for the ancestral traditions of white native and white immigrant subcultures, which are alleged by overclass intellectuals to be hopelessly tainted by white supremacy or colonialism.[16] This is plausible in the case of celebrations of the pro-slavery Confederacy by white southerners in the United States. But America's Columbus Day holiday, named for a famous Italian, was established as an affirmation of pride in the heritage of working-class Italian Americans who had long suffered from the contempt of elite Anglo-American Protestants. It is not, as today's sanctimonious overclass left claims, a celebration of the brutal policies of Columbus toward native Americans in the Caribbean. Needless to say, the double standard of Western establishments when it comes to sentiments of ancestral pride provides recruits for racial and cultural nativism and demagogic populism.

Another cultural clash among members of the overclass and the working class within native white majorities in America and Europe involves family relationships and local attachments or the lack of them. The British thinker David Goodhart has contrasted the communitarian localism of less-educated "Somewheres" with the individualistic careerism of educated "Anywheres."[17] For many working-class Somewheres, personal identities as members of particular local communities or extended families are more important than their low-status jobs. In contrast, Goodhart's Anywheres, educated and mobile members of the managerial overclass, often think of themselves as "citizens of the world"; derive their personal status from their prestigious occupations, not their local or national communities; abandon their low-status class or ethnic or regional accents in order to succeed in metropolitan careers; and jettison ancestral traditions in favor of ever-changing transnational elite fashions.

To members of the overclass accustomed to thinking of

geographic mobility in the interest of a professional career as the norm, it may come as a shock to learn that the average American lives within eighteen miles of her mother. Fifty-seven percent of Americans have never lived outside of their home states and 37 percent have spent their entire lives in their hometowns, with the exception of periods of military service or college education.[18] Those without a university degree are far less likely to travel across the country or the world in pursuit of career goals. The numbers are similar in Europe.

Reflecting the sacrifice of family commitments to career ambitions that is characteristic of many highly educated and ambitious overclass professionals, a survey of twenty-four advanced industrial democracies showed that, compared to the non-college-educated, university-educated individuals are more likely to describe children as a "burden" rather than as a "joy."[19] Working-class households are far more likely than overclass households to rely on a stay-at-home parent or relatives to care for children. In the United States, 66 percent of those whose education ended with high school say that children are better off when one parent stays at home to raise them; the number plunges to 51 percent for those with a bachelor's degree or more.[20]

Urban hubs increasingly are populated by individuals without any children at all. According to the American Community Survey, in 2016 there were more dogs than children in San Francisco.[21] Writing in *The Atlantic* in 2019, Derek Thompson concluded: "The Future of the City Is Childless."[22]

ALTHOUGH RACISM IS declining, racist attitudes linger in the US and Europe, following centuries of institutionalized white supremacy that came to an end only in the mid-twentieth century. Racial and ethnic bigotry undoubtedly motivate the opposition of some voters to immigration.

But if bigotry were the sole or major factor inspiring native workers to oppose high levels of immigration, native white working-class citizens in the West should be as hostile to affluent and educated nonwhite immigrants as they are to low-wage nonwhite immigrants. But this is not the case. In the US, attitudes toward immigration are chiefly determined by class; less-skilled workers are more likely to favor immigration restriction than more-educated workers.[23] At the same time, there is broad cross-class support in the US and other Western countries in favor of skilled rather than unskilled immigration.[24] In the US there has been no significant backlash against East Asian and South Asian immigrants, who tend to be college-educated professionals, comparable to the backlash against less-skilled and disproportionately poor Latin American immigrants, even though Asian immigrants are nonwhite as well. In Britain, working-class populists have complained about "Polish plumbers" and other lower-income immigrants from Central and Eastern Europe who are white. As split labor market theory would predict, the native working-class backlash has been greatest against particular groups of immigrants, nonwhite or white, who are viewed as competitors for jobs or welfare and public services.

T HE GEOGRAPHIC POLARIZATION that is evident in Western democracies, then, reflects the social divide among classes who live in different areas—college-educated overclasses and the disproportionately immigrant working poor in the high-density hubs and the mostly native, mostly white working classes in the low-density heartlands. Their differences over environmental policy, trade, immigration, and other issues reflect conflicting interests, values, lifestyles, and aspirations.

Can today's new class war, fought on all of these different fronts at once, give way to a new class peace? The history of the last century in the West provides some hope. By the middle of the twentieth century, the first class war between the managerial overclass and the working class came to an end in an uneasy cross-class peace that lasted for a generation. While it lasted, the democracies of Europe and North America enjoyed the greatest expansion of mass prosperity and civil rights in their histories.

How class war gave way to class peace nearly a century ago in the West is the subject of the next chapter.

CHAPTER THREE

World Wars and New Deals

To UNDERSTAND HOW the new class war in the West came to be, it is necessary to understand how the old class war came to an end.

The first class war of the modern era had its origins in the growth of industrial capitalism in the nineteenth and twentieth centuries. In different Western countries, industrialization proceeded at different rates and took different forms. But everywhere the social challenges were similar.

The American economist John Bates Clark observed in 1901: "If the carboniferous age were to return and the earth were to repeople itself with dinosaurs, the change that would be made in animal life would scarcely seem greater than that which had been made in business life by these monster-like corporations."[1] The great merger movement of 1895–1904 in the US created huge firms in many industries, including some that still exist, like DuPont, Nabisco, International Harvester, and Otis Elevator. By 1900, more than four hundred US manufacturing establishments—half of them in the iron or steel and textile industries—employed more than a thousand workers each.[2]

Unable personally to supervise huge concerns and enormous workforces, capitalists were forced to rely on a new kind of professional, the managers, who increasingly were trained in scientific management at newly founded business schools. In one sector of the economy after another, mass production by workers using advanced machinery replaced small-scale craft production by artisans. The mechanization of agriculture destroyed the livelihoods and communities of tenants and family farmers. Around smoke-spewing factories, shantytowns of workers grew, spawning crises of sanitation, health, and crime. Migrations of rural natives and foreign immigrants to factory jobs in industrial towns produced ethnic clashes and political backlashes.

The US, as it replaced Britain as the most advanced industrial capitalist economy in the world, was the site of some of the worst labor violence, with government and business frequently allied to crush workers in the era from the Civil War to the 1930s. Homestead, Ludlow, the Battle of Blair Mountain—these were the equivalents of the Battle of Bunker Hill and Yorktown and Antietam and Gettysburg in the first American class war.

I N THE NINETEENTH and early twentieth centuries, five major schools of thought debated the future of industrial society: liberalism, producerism, socialism, corporatism, and pluralism. Economic liberalism has come in several varieties, including the eclectic and flexible "classical liberalism" of Adam Smith, David Ricardo, and J. S. Mill and a more rigidly antistatist ideology, associated with Friedrich Hayek and Ludwig von Mises and Milton Friedman and already called "neoliberalism" by the 1920s. In all its forms, economic liberalism identifies human freedom with commercial transactions in markets, with the state limited to the role of enforcing contracts and perhaps providing minimal social insurance safety nets. Free market liberals tend to view national boundaries as unfortunate and anachronistic barriers to the free movement of capital and workers in a single global market economy.[3]

Capitalist and managerial elites in the West have often promoted versions of economic liberalism, from the classical liberalism of the early nineteenth century to the globalist neoliberalism of today. In different ways, producerism, socialism, corporatism, and pluralism have rejected the liberal ideal that the economy should be governed on the basis of maximum flexibility for businesses in a free market for labor as well as other inputs to production.

Producerism is the belief that the economy should be structured by the state to maximize the numbers of self-employed family farmers, artisans, and small shopkeepers in society. The moral ideal of this school is the self-sufficient citizen of a republic with a small-producer majority whose economic independence means that they cannot be intimidated or blackmailed by wealthy elites. In the form of Jeffersonian agrarianism, producerism has a rich history in the United States. The rise of mass production in the economy, and the shift from a majority made up of farm owners and farm workers to urban wage earners, rendered the producerist ideal irrelevant in the modern industrialized West. While small-producerism still has appeal to romantics on both the left and the right, it is and will remain anachronistic, and having criticized it elsewhere, I will not discuss it in this book.[4]

Socialists of various kinds—utopian, Christian, and Marxist—denounced capitalism and private property and proposed public ownership of industry and infrastructure. By the early 1900s, the Marxist school itself had split into several squabbling sects. Revolutionary Marxist-Leninist communists seized power in Russia in 1917 and in China in 1949; by the 1970s their tyrannical regimes ruled a third of the human race. So-called revisionist Marxists favored working for peaceful reform through democratic systems and influenced moderate social democratic parties in Western Europe. Revolutionary syndicalists rejected liberal democracy for militant violence and influenced the fascist ideology of Italy's Benito Mussolini, a former socialist.[5]

A fourth philosophy, opposed to free market liberalism and state socialism alike, envisioned a harmonious society of state-supervised but largely self-governing "corporations," by which was meant entire economic sectors, not individual firms, rather like medieval guilds.[6] This tradition influenced Catholic social thought, as expressed in the papal encyclicals *Rerum novarum* (1891) and *Quadragesimo anno* (1931). For the French sociologist Émile Durkheim and others in the secular French republican solidarist tradition, the organization of labor and business could be an antidote to "anomie," a phrase Durkheim devised to describe the isolation and disorientation of many individuals in urban industrial societies.[7]

The same term, "corporatism," is often used for both democratic and dictatorial versions of this political tradition.

Political scientists have distinguished authoritarian "state" corporatism from "societal" or "social" corporatism, which is compatible with democracy and civil liberties.[8] But apart from favoring a few institutions like tripartite business-labor-government negotiations in some industries, so-called state corporatism and social corporatism have little to do with each other. The view of society as a community of self-organized and self-governing communities, under the supervision of a democratic government, is best described as "pluralism," the term used by the English pluralists of the early twentieth century, like Neville Figgis, F. W. Maitland, G. D. H. Cole, and Harold Laski, and by their late-twentieth-century heirs, including Paul Hirst and David Marquand.[9]

In the early 1900s, the "national efficiency" school in the UK had affinities with pluralism and, in its more militaristic versions, with state corporatism. The members of the national efficiency school included Fabian socialists like Sidney and Beatrice Webb and conservative imperialists like the editor Leopold Maxse, along with the novelist H. G. Wells. Despite their differences on many issues, all believed that social reform along with rearmament was necessary to maintain Britain's role in the world, which was threatened by the rise of Imperial Germany.[10]

Arguments like those of the national efficiency school ultimately prevailed in many Western democracies. British prime minister Lloyd George championed social reforms in 1917 in the midst of World War I on the grounds that "you cannot maintain an A-1 empire with a C-3 population."[11] During the two world wars and the Great Depression of the twentieth century, the deciding vote among competing models of industrial society in the West was cast by war.

IN MUCH OF EUROPE, World War I was a catalyst for an increased role in economic security and social provision by the state. During and immediately after the war, Britain created ministries of Labour (1916), Reconstruction (1917), and Health (1919). Lloyd George proposed a program of public housing to build "homes fit for heroes." In France, fear that low fertility might cause military insecurity helped to inspire support for family allowances. In the case of the democratic Weimar Republic in Germany after World War I, the political scientist Gunther Mai observes: "With the exception of the eight-hour day, there is no important social policy innovation in the Weimar Republic that had not been already introduced during wartime on the basis of social rights: unemployment benefits, short-time working benefit, child allowances, labour exchanges, even de facto a sort of minimum wage."[12]

After the US entered World War I, the US government adopted wartime corporatism, organizing the economy for military production under dozens of "commodity sections," under the leadership of the War Industries Board (WIB). To avert strikes that might disrupt war production and transportation, the Wilson administration acted as a broker in labor-management relations through the National War Labor Board. Trade union leaders were appointed along with business executives to the Advisory Commission to the Council of National Defense, the War Industries Board, the Railroad Administration, and other agencies. Thanks to pro-union government policy, between 1913 and 1920 union membership in the US increased by 85 percent.[13]

Herbert Hoover, the acclaimed head of the Food Administration during the war, became commerce secretary from 1921 to 1928 and president from 1929 to 1933. Although he claimed to be a free market liberal, Hoover supported high tariffs and favored a purely voluntary system of business-labor cooperation known as "associationalism," under which businesses would maintain high wages and unions would avoid strikes. But wartime trade union gains in the US were reversed by a postwar business offensive against organized labor, and during the Great Depression that began in 1929 many paternalistic employer welfare programs collapsed.

Following his election in 1932, President Franklin Delano Roosevelt, who had served as assistant secretary of the navy under President Woodrow Wilson, sought to revive the US economy by means of a peacetime version of wartime mobilization. The Reconstruction Finance Corporation, created under Hoover and expanded under FDR, was a reincarnation of the War Finance Corporation of World War I, just as the Securities and Exchange Commission was inspired by the World War I–era Capital Issues Committee.

The most important agency inspired by earlier wartime collaboration among business, unions, and government was the National Industrial Recovery Administration, later renamed the National Recovery Administration (NRA), created by the National Industrial Recovery Act (NIRA) of Congress in 1933. Not only was the NRA modeled on the War Industries Board of World War I, but also it was led by

General Hugh Johnson, who had worked for the financier Bernard Baruch, the head of the WIB. Under NRA supervision, industries were organized into government-supervised, self-regulating sectors similar to the commodity sections of World War I. With government approval, in return for exemption from antitrust laws, businesses in each sector were to draw up industry-wide codes of conduct, which included sectoral minimum wages. Under section 7(a) of the NIRA, inspired by the wartime model of the National War Labor Board, each industry code had to guarantee labor's "right to organize and bargain collectively through representatives of their own choosing."[14]

In 1935 the NRA was abolished when the Supreme Court struck down its enabling legislation, on the technical grounds that Congress had delegated too much authority to the president. But the wreckage of the NRA was plundered to construct a system that structured the US economy from the 1930s to the 1970s. NRA industry codes were reborn as regulations in commission-governed industries like aviation, trucking, and coal, which were treated as public utilities. Instead of the sectoral minimum wages and working hours and pensions that were to have been agreed on in each industry by business and labor and ratified by the NRA, the federal government directly imposed a one-size-fits-all national minimum wage and eight-hour day in 1938, in addition to the federal Social Security program that was enacted earlier in 1935. The Wagner Act of 1935 turned section 7(a) of the National Industrial Recovery Act into the statute that, as amended, governs collective bargaining in the United States to this day.

DURING WORLD WAR II, many Western governments promised their soldiers and workers a better life after the Axis alliance of National Socialist Germany, Fascist Italy, and Imperial Japan was defeated. In Britain the Beveridge Report, calling for a massive expansion of welfare services for the working class, was published in November 1942 and helped to inspire the postwar National Health Service.

In his State of the Union address of January 11, 1944, President Roosevelt called for a Second Bill of Rights, explicitly linking promises of new rights to jobs, adequate wages, homes, medical care, education, and other goods to the wartime effort: "It is our duty now to begin to lay the plans and determine the strategy for the winning of a lasting peace and the establishment of an American standard of living higher than ever before known. . . . And after this war is won we must be prepared to move forward, in the implementation of these rights, to new goals of human happiness and well-being." FDR's Second Bill of Rights was more an aspiration than a proposal, but its spirit was embodied in the GI Bill (of Rights), passed by the US Congress in 1944. The war effort accelerated reform in other areas, including the tentative beginnings of the federal role in dismantling racial segregation.

The greatest gains for organized labor in American history came during World War II. Using the leverage of defense spending, the War Labor Board enacted a "maintenance of membership" rule mandating that all new employees in a unionized plant belong to the union. Membership in the

United Steelworkers grew from 225,000 (in 1939) to 708,000 by 1944, while membership in the United Auto Workers ballooned from 165,000 in 1939 to more than a million.[15] More than 35 percent of the nonagricultural labor force was unionized by 1945.

To one degree or another, every economy in Western Europe and North America after 1945 was based on tripartite economic bargaining, of a kind compatible with representative democracy, as opposed to the authoritarian state corporatism adopted by interwar fascist regimes and by dictatorships in Spain, Portugal, and Latin America. In a democratic pluralist system, occupational representation does not replace representative democracy based on free elections of representatives from territorial districts or the country as a whole. But the unregulated labor market is partly replaced by a state-brokered system of bargaining over wages and working conditions among employers or employer associations and independent trade unions or other labor organizations.[16]

Elaborate forms of national sectoral bargaining among employers and labor unions were created in postwar Sweden and Austria. In the Federal Republic of Germany, collective bargaining was supplemented by codetermination, the practice of having union representatives on the boards of large corporations. In France, union membership has always been relatively low, but the results of employer-union bargaining have covered great numbers of workers. One study notes: "The shadows of Fascism and/or foreign threat were decisive or at least significant in all the most successful and enduring peace settlements."[17]

The labor historian Nelson Lichtenstein points out: "Building upon the framework established by the National War Labor Board, the big industrial unions settled into a postwar collective-bargaining routine that increased real weekly wages some 50% in the next two decades and greatly expanded their fringe benefit welfare packages."[18] Following the Treaty of Detroit in 1950—a five-year contract negotiated by the United Auto Workers with General Motors—and similar deals, the US had a de facto system of democratic corporatism in its concentrated manufacturing sector, which by means of "pattern bargaining" informally set standards for wages and benefits in many nonunionized sectors. Union membership in the US peaked in the 1950s at around a third of the workforce. Meanwhile, the long-struggling farm sector was stabilized and integrated with government by means of a system of price supports and subsidies.

While many business executives continued to grumble, on both sides of the Atlantic the legitimacy of labor-capital bargaining was accepted by mainstream conservatives as well as progressives. Dwight Eisenhower told his brother Edgar: "Should any political party attempt to abolish Social Security, unemployment insurance, and eliminate labor laws and farm programs, you would not hear of that party again in our political history."[19] The historian Robert Griffith notes the sources of Eisenhower's vision of what Griffith calls a "corporate commonwealth": "Common to all of these activities was an attempt to fashion a new corporative economy that would avoid both the destructive disorder of unregulated capitalism and the threat to business autonomy posed by socialism."[20]

I N POLITICS, THE equivalents of strong unions in the post–
World War II era in North America and Europe were
mass-membership parties. Despite the beginnings of subur-
banization, national politicians were still connected with local
voters by several layers of regional, urban, and neighborhood
party officials—urban "bosses" and rural "courthouse gangs"
in the United States. Intellectuals tended to sneer at these provincial power brokers, some of whom were indeed ignorant or
corrupt or racist. But the existence of this layer of petty tribunes ensured that politicians would not ignore the interests
and values of local working-class constituencies in local, state,
and national politics.

The democratic pluralism of the New Deal was reflected
in the very structure of post-1945 American government.
Early-twentieth-century American progressives like Woodrow Wilson had combined their contempt for legislators
with idealization of altruistic, nonpartisan civil servants,
protected from political interference, who would apply expertise in social science to the making of policy in the public
interest.

Whether they were supporters or opponents of New Deal
liberal policies, southern Democrats and northern Catholics
in the dominant New Deal Democratic coalition refused to
increase the discretionary power of elite federal bureaucrats
who would probably be recruited disproportionately from
the educated Protestant upper middle class of the North and
Midwest and educated at a handful of Ivy League universities.
Successive plans for executive reorganization, which would

have put the president in charge of a rationalized continental European–style administrative state, never made it through Congress. Agrarian populists, sometimes allied with organized labor in the factory cities, sought to expand the capacities of the federal government in key areas, while avoiding the creation of a European-style generalist civil service with substantial independent policy-making authority. They achieved their goal by the creation of sector-specific agencies like the US Department of Agriculture and the Civil Aeronautics Board with narrow mandates that worked closely with a sector's stakeholders, including in some cases farm organizations and unions. A necessary corollary of this approach was judicial deference to the decisions of Congress and congressionally supervised federal agencies.[21]

The system that emerged in the US by the 1940s came to be known as "interest group liberalism," a pluralist system in which public policy emerged from negotiations among economic interest groups, each with its own power brokers, rather than from a technocratic mandarinate of all-wise, altruistic experts insulated from popular pressure, or from the "invisible hand" of the free market.

IN THE REALM of culture or civil society, including the mass media and education, as well as in the economy and politics, a system of democratic pluralism that empowered the working class coalesced in the United States and other Western democracies in the mid-twentieth century. The clergy and zealous citizens and civic groups policed the mass media and the educational system to ensure that they did not offend the largely traditional values of the working-class majority.

Beginning in 1933, the National Legion of Decency, organized by Catholics, won the privilege of having Hollywood films submitted for their approval or condemnation. Meanwhile, in suburbs and small towns, Protestant "church ladies" scoured public libraries and school libraries for books they considered subversive and obscene. Often they invited the derision of metropolitan elites with campaigns to ban literary classics like J. D. Salinger's *Catcher in the Rye*. But these parochial and provincial activists undoubtedly represented the values and views of large numbers of Americans, who in their absence, as today, would have been passive recipients of whatever content distant commercial media corporations in Los Angeles or New York chose to offer in a media market that rewarded sensationalism, obscenity, and violence.

In the Western democracies, Catholics played a role out of proportion to their numbers in postwar democratic systems. Germany's Christian Democrats were inspired by Catholic social thought with its strong prolabor and corporatist themes, and so were the founders of the early European Common Market. In the United States, the lesser power brokers who acted as tribunes of the urban white working class—political bosses, trade union officials, and clergy—were disproportionately Catholic.

Paradoxical as it might seem, the assimilation and integration of first- and second-generation European Catholic immigrants into the American mainstream was undoubtedly hastened by the low levels of immigration in the US between World War I and the 1960s. Low levels of immigration and limited opportunities for offshoring were necessary, but not sufficient, conditions for the growth of working-class bargaining power and prosperity in the generation after 1945. This is not to defend the racist national origins quotas of the US in the 1920s, which built on earlier proscriptions of Asian immigration and privileged Northern European over other European nationalities. It is merely to point out that it would have been practically impossible to organize and maintain labor unions or mobilize public support for New Deal–style social programs in the middle of the twentieth century, if immigration had continued at the levels that existed in the early 1900s and again today.

IN THE DEMOCRATIC pluralist era after World War II, working-class majorities managed to increase their bargaining power in the economy, government, and the culture alike. What John Kenneth Galbraith called the "countervailing power" of groups that pooled their resources to strengthen their bargaining positions was at the core of the New Deal in America and similar social settlements in postwar Europe.[22] The legal scholar William Forbath has written:

Recalling the Jacksonians' core anti-oligarchy insight, that the laboring "many" needed mass organizations with the clout to counter the wealthy "few," New Dealers declared that their labor law reforms would come to the republic's rescue by finally "incorporat[ing] the industrial workers in the polity of the United States" as a "check upon the power of 'Big Business.'" Just as Jacksonians defended the invention of the mass party as a structural constitutional necessity, so New Dealers defended the invention of the industrial union.[23]

In 1940 in his book *The American Stakes*, the journalist John Chamberlain, a supporter of the New Deal who later became a conservative, criticized traditional progressive and populist ideas of a unitary public or national interest: "The individual, under idealist theory, must bow when the Committee of the Whole speaks." Chamberlain contrasted this kind of centralization with the democratic pluralism of the New Deal:

> The labor union, the consumers' or producers' cooperative, the "institute," the syndicate—these are the important things in a democracy. If their power is evenly spread, if there are economic checks and balances to parallel the political checks and balances, then society will be democratic. For democracy is what results when you have a state of tension in society that permits no one group to dare bid for the total power.

Noting that "Communists will call this a reactionary position," Chamberlain argued that on the contrary the New Deal sought to balance corporate power: "For the labor union and the co-operative still lag far behind the business institute and syndicate in power; they must be built up."[24] In addition, according to Chamberlain, the New Deal "was designed primarily to even things up between the plutocratic city and the impoverished country, between metropolitan East and plundered West and South."

In this vision of democratic pluralism as an alternative to both dictatorship and plutocracy, leadership was exerted by those whom Chamberlain called "broker-politicians" like FDR who presided over compromises among "bosses" representing various important economic and social groups: "Indeed, the pressure group, far from being the loathsome thing that it is commonly accounted by the philosophical idealist, is absolutely necessary to the functioning of an industrial democracy. . . . Unlovely as the boss is in some of his tactics, you can't have a world of freedom without him: the right of a group to political broker-service is the only practicable alternative to the Gestapo and the concentration camp."[25]

FOLLOWING WORLD WAR II, free market liberals of the kind called "neoliberals" or "libertarians," like Ludwig von Mises and Friedrich Hayek, insisted that the West could no longer be considered economically liberal. They were right. Even the most business-friendly postwar democracies like the US and Britain and West Germany had mixed economies characterized by forms of labor-business bargaining and economic regulation and public spending that would have been politically impossible before the Great Depression and World War II. Under the postwar Bretton Woods system, exchange rates were controlled and capital controls in Western Europe were not relaxed until the late 1950s.

The first class war in the industrial West between the managerial overclass and the working class ended after 1945 with national class compromises like the New Deal in the US, designed to buy social peace first during wartime mobilization and then in postwar economic recovery by incorporating formerly marginalized workers and family farmers into the national power structure. Democratic pluralism in North America and Europe, an alternative to the extremes of free market liberalism, socialism, and state corporatism, compelled the representatives of national overclasses to share power and bargain with lesser elites who acted as power brokers for working-class communities in the three realms of the economy, government, and culture.

By the 1950s, a new democratic pluralist dispensation, built to a large degree on wartime institutions and reforms, existed in the US and Western Europe. The details differed in Eisenhower's America, de Gaulle's France, and Adenauer's Germany. But everywhere in the democratic West, class conflict between managerial elites in the economy, government, and the media and education was limited and channeled into institutionalized negotiations.

In the US and elsewhere, campaigns for the legal and political equality of racial and ethnic minorities took a generation longer to succeed. But democratic government in the Western nations had been stabilized by the integration of two groups—urban labor and family farmers—that had been marginalized and exploited in the early stages of managerial capitalism. In one Western country after another, the need to mobilize conscripts and workers for war and the fear of a return to Depression-spawned radicalism had compelled the managerial overclass reluctantly to cut "new deals" with national working classes. The results were unprecedented levels of working-class prosperity and economic growth during what in France was called *les Trente Glorieuses*, the "thirty glorious years" that followed 1945.

But the war-inspired class peace treaties within Western democracies would not last. For many members of the managerial overclass, the need to share power, wealth, and cultural authority with petty tribunes of the working class like trade union officials and small-town politicians and religious leaders was an indignity to be endured only under duress, until they could liberate themselves from constraint.

CHAPTER FOUR

The Neoliberal Revolution from Above

T HE CLASS PEACE BETWEEN Western overclasses and Western working classes was never more than a temporary armistice. Economic neoliberals like Friedrich Hayek and Milton Friedman gathered in annual retreats in Mont-Pèlerin in Switzerland to dream of the overthrow of the new regime and the establishment of a global free market utopia. Marginalized by postwar "middlebrow" culture, with its deference to traditional and religious working-class sensibilities, cultural liberals found their own redoubts—the bohemias of the Left Bank of the Seine and San Francisco and Greenwich Village and countless college campuses with enrollments swelled by veterans and their children.

By the turn of the twenty-first century, thanks to what the social critic Christopher Lasch called "the revolt of the elites," democratic pluralism in the Atlantic democracies had been overthrown and replaced by the current regime of technocratic neoliberalism—the new orthodoxy of the credentialed managerial overclass whose members simultaneously dominate the governments, corporate suites, universities, foundations, and media of the Western world. Neoliberalism is a synthesis of the free market economic liberalism of the libertarian right and the cultural liberalism of the bohemian/ academic left. Its economic model, based on global tax, regulatory, and labor arbitrage, weakens both democratic nation-states and national working-class majorities. Its preferred model of government is apolitical, anti-majoritarian, elitist, and technocratic.

IN THE ECONOMIC REALM, the revolution from above began in the 1970s. An intellectual and political insurgency treated institutions like tripartite business-labor-government wage setting, trade unions, and the regulation of industries as public utilities as obstacles to both economic progress and individual liberty. On the overclass right, such institutions were denounced by libertarian economists as "crony capitalism" and by conservative constitutional lawyers in the United States as infringements on the supposed quasi-royalist "unitary power" of the president. On the overclass left, many of the same structures were demonized by public interest progressives like Ralph Nader whose constituency consisted of affluent and educated reformers.[1] The political scientist Theodore Lowi coined the term "interest group liberalism" for New Deal arrangements as an insult.[2]

By 1986, a bipartisan consensus among American intellectuals and policy makers held that inherited democratic pluralist institutions were both corrupt and inefficient. The journalist Nicholas Lemann felt obliged to explain why New

Dealers had supported interest group liberalism in the first place:

> To understand this as a heartfelt position, you have to imagine how the world looked to liberals in the 1940s. . . . [Franklin Roosevelt] had consistently ignored the systematic advice of the left, and instead adopted an inconsistent patchwork of programs designed to fix specific problems—and it saved the country. . . . Arguments made on behalf of the general interest of all citizens seemed much more suspicious then than now, because they had been the province of Stalinists and ideologists of pure capitalism at home and of Hitler and Mussolini abroad. . . . There was also, again almost unimaginably more than in these times of populist politics, a great mistrust of "mass man" on the part of the American establishment a generation ago. Demagogues might use mass communications to stir up fascism in the general public, but the wise leaders of interest groups, who would ignore "the cosmic enthusiasms of individual men" (Boorstin again), could operate a consensus state that would be good for everyone.[3]

By the time Lemann wrote that, the emerging orthodoxy shared from center-left to center-right held that Western countries would be more just and efficient if only enlightened technocratic policy makers and dynamic corporate executives could be liberated from the power of elected politicians and organized labor. In 1975 Michel Crozier, Samuel P. Huntington, and Joji Watanuki wrote a report for the elite Trilateral Commission, *The Crisis of Democracy: On the Governability of Democracies*, which was published as a book. In Europe, the US, and Japan, the authors concluded, major problems "stem from an excess of democracy." In 1997 former Federal Reserve vice chairman Alan Blinder, a neoliberal Democrat, asked: "Do we want to take more policy decisions out of the realm of politics and put them in the realm of technocracy?" Blinder suggested that tax policy, trade policy, and environmental policy might be delegated to independent technocratic agencies, with only minimal congressional control.[4] In 2019, Cass Sunstein, who had been the head of the Office of Information and Regulatory Affairs from 2009 to 2012, during the Obama administration, suggested that the US was afflicted by excessive "partyism," for which the cure "lies in delegation, and in particular in strengthening the hand of technocratic forces in government."[5]

Economic activities that could not be insulated from democratic meddling by transferring them to technocratic government agencies could be transferred wholly to private sector elites by privatization and marketization. In the United States, Jimmy Carter, not Ronald Reagan, was the first president of the post–New Deal neoliberal era. Beginning with Carter's presidency, a number of industries that had been regulated during the New Deal were deregulated by Congress: airlines (1978), rail (1980), trucking (1980), busing (1982), telecommunications (1996, 1999).

While deregulation improved performance in some industries, in others, like home mortgage lending and finance, deregulation led to widespread abuses that helped to inflate the asset bubbles that burst in the Great Recession. Moreover, deregulation in many sectors led to the collapse of many private sector unions, which had been bulwarks of the prosperous working class, called "the middle class" in the United States. Similar deregulatory reforms and anti-union measures were adopted by many European governments, including those of center-left leaders like Tony Blair and Gerhard Schröder, following the example of free market conservatives like British prime minister Margaret Thatcher.

Neoliberal economic reforms initially were justified as a response to the "stagflation" (combined stagnation and inflation) that afflicted Europe and North America in the 1970s. While the oil shocks of the 1970s contributed to the problem, in hindsight there were several structural causes: slower productivity growth as a result of the exhaustion of the technological possibilities of the earlier electromechanical revolution, before the benefits of the information technology (IT) revolution had become important; pressure on corporate profits from overproduction in manufacturing, caused by the postwar recovery of Germany and Japan and their export-oriented manufacturing strategies; and pressure on profits as well from trade unions enabled by tight, low-immigration labor markets to demand wage increases outstripping productivity growth, which fueled wage-push inflation.

At the time, a number of Western thinkers and policy makers, mostly on the center-left, favored encouraging wage restraint on the part of unions by means of tripartite business-labor-government social compacts, combined with national industrial strategies to boost technology-driven productivity growth. This strategic response to stagflation would have modernized the postwar social contract. If successful, it would have boosted productivity growth, profits, and wages at the same time.

Instead, neoliberal policy makers in the US and Europe chose to dismantle the basic structures of the post-1945 system, weakening organized labor in the private sector and boosting corporate profits by means of short-term global arbitrage instead of government-assisted technological innovation and investment at home. Enriching the few and enraging the many, the neoliberal cure for the stagflation of the 1970s was worse than the disease.

THE MOVE AWAY from regulation and the weakening of organized labor at home helped to boost corporate profit margins. So did global arbitrage—the strategy of taking advantage of differences in wages, regulations, or taxes among different political jurisdictions in the world or among states or provinces in a federal nation-state.

Tax arbitrage is the practice by which firms take advantage of differences in tax rates and subsidies in different countries in order to similarly boost profits without boosting productivity. The former chief economist of McKinsey & Company, James S. Henry, has estimated that roughly one-fourth of all the world's wealth is held in tax havens.[6] According to the Congressional Research Service, in 2015 US-based multinationals recorded 43 percent of their foreign earnings as taking place in five tax havens—Bermuda, Ireland, Luxembourg, the Netherlands, and Switzerland— which accounted for only 4 percent of their workforces.[7] A single office building in Grand Cayman, named Ugland House, is the registered legal address of 18,557 companies.[8]

Even as they have exploited opportunities for international tax arbitrage, firms and lobbies in the post–Cold War era of globalization have also promoted regulatory arbitrage, the selective harmonization of laws and rules, when it has been in their interest to do so.

In the second half of the twentieth century, successive rounds of negotiation under the auspices of the General Agreement on Tariffs and Trade (GATT) and, more recently, the World Trade Organization (WTO) effectively reduced most traditional tariff barriers. By 2016, when the WTO effectively terminated the failed Doha Development Round of global trade talks, the United States and other leading industrial nations had shifted the emphasis from removing barriers restricting the cross-border flow of goods to harmonizing laws and regulations through "multiregional trade pacts," like the North American Free Trade Agreement (NAFTA), the Trans-Pacific Partnership (TPP), and the Transatlantic Trade and Investment Partnership (TTIP), in the interests of transnational investors and corporations reliant on transnational supply chains.

The economic sectors chosen by Western governments for arbitrage and harmonization reflect the interests not of national working-class majorities but of national managerial elites. Harmonizing labor standards or wages would undercut the corporate search for the cheapest labor, while transnational crackdowns on tax avoidance would thwart the strategy of tax arbitrage by transnational firms. Instead, the emphasis in harmonization policy has been on common industrial standards, the liberalization of financial systems, and intellectual property rights, including pharmaceutical patents. These kinds of harmonization benefit transnational firms, investors on Wall Street or in the City of London, and the holders of intellectual property rights in Silicon Valley and the pharmaceutical industry.

In many cases, this kind of regulatory harmonization makes sense—standardizing product safety measures or supply chain specifications, for example. But the new regulatory harmonization agreements produce a democratic deficit by removing whole areas of regulation from the realm of ordinary legislation. Laws and regulations that corporate lobbyists are unable to persuade national democratic legislatures to enact can be repackaged and hidden in harmonization agreements masked as lengthy trade treaties, which are then ratified by legislatures without adequate scrutiny. Whatever its minor benefits, legislation by treaty represents a massive transfer of power from democratic legislatures to corporate managers and bankers. Jean-Claude Juncker, the prime minister of the tax haven Luxembourg who became the president of the European Commission from 2014 to 2019, described how the European Council systematically expanded its authority by stealth: "We decree something, then float it and wait some time to see what happens. If no clamor occurs . . . because most people do not grasp what had been decided, we continue—step by step, until the point of no return is reached."[9]

B Y FAR THE most important form of arbitrage strategy employed by Western-based corporations has been global labor arbitrage. In 2003 the economist Stephen Roach popularized the term:

> In an era of excess supply, companies lack pricing leverage as never before. As such, businesses must be unrelenting in their search for new efficiencies. Not surprisingly, the primary focus of such efforts is labor, representing the bulk of production costs in the developed world; in the US, for example, worker compensation still makes up nearly 80% of total domestic corporate income. And that's the point: Wage rates in China and India range from 10% to 25% of those for comparable-quality workers in the US and the rest of the developed world. Consequently, offshore outsourcing that extracts product from relatively low-wage workers in the developing world has become an increasingly urgent survival tactic for companies in the developed economies.[10]

In 2012, the McKinsey Global Institute (MGI) concluded that from 1980 to 2010 1.7 billion workers joined the global labor force.[11] In a 2019 report, MGI downplayed global labor cost arbitrage, claiming that it accounted for only 18 percent of goods trade. MGI derived this low number by redefining labor arbitrage as "exports from countries whose GDP per capita is one-fifth or less than that of the importing country." By this offshoring-friendly definition, if a firm shuts down a factory in the US (GDP per capita in 2017: $59,500 in purchasing power parity) and opens a factory with much cheaper workers in China ($16,700) or Indonesia ($12,400) or Venezuela ($12,100), the resulting exports to the US market are "not from a low-wage country to a high-wage country."[12] In contrast with MGI, the Nobel laureate economist Michael Spence claims that "labor arbitrage has been the core driver of global supply chains for at least three decades—with significant distributional and employment effects."[13]

According to the Commerce Department, between 1999 and 2009 US multinational corporations cut 864,600 workers in the US while adding 2.9 million workers abroad. Fifty-seven percent of the foreign hiring by nonfinancial companies was in Asia, with multinationals adding 683,000 workers in China and 392,000 workers in India. In the same period, multinationals cut capital-investment spending in the US by 0.2 percent a year, while increasing it abroad by 4 percent a year.[14] These foreign workforces included much low-wage labor on goods and services for export, or reexport, to the US or Europe. The global profits of many Western managers and investors depend in large part on the labor of poor women in foreign sweatshops, as Delia Aquilar observes: "From the maquiladoras in Mexico . . . to assembly plants and export processing zones [EPZs] in Central America, the Caribbean, and the Pacific Rim, to subcontractors and garment sweatshops in global cities and in nations of the periphery, it is women's labor that allows and guarantees maximum profitability for the corporate elite, a tiny minority of the world's inhabitants."[15]

The economist David Autor and several coauthors have shown that "the China shock"—the flood of Chinese imports into the US following China's entry into the WTO—did far more damage to US manufacturing employment than the previous consensus had held, destroying 2 million to 2.4 million net jobs in manufacturing and manufacturing-related industries between 1999 and 2011 and contributing to the "employment sag" in the US in that period.[16] A study in 2013 by Michael W. L. Elsby, Bart Hobijn, and Aysegul Sahin concluded that "increases in the import exposure of US businesses can account for 3.3 percentage points of the 3.9 percentage point decline in the US payroll share over the past quarter century."[17]

AMONG MULTINATIONAL FIRMS, Apple in particular has mastered the arts of tax, regulatory, and labor arbitrage. Through subcontractors, Apple employs Chinese workers to assemble most of its iPhones and iPads for wages and under working conditions that would be illegal in the US or any Western democracy. According to Konstantin Kakaes in *MIT Technology Review*, producing every single component of the iPhone in the United States, in addition to assembling it in the United States, would at most add $100 to the cost of the device.[18] But while domestic production would not seriously inconvenience American consumers, American labor costs might cut into Apple's profit margin, which in 2010 was 59 percent of the final sales price of its iPhone 4, with labor costs in China accounting for only 1.8 percent.[19] In 2017, Apple's iPhone X, which cost $357.50 to make and sold for $999, gave Apple a gross profit margin of 64 percent.[20]

To avoid taxation, according to a US Senate subcommittee in 2013, Apple has used a variety of tax arbitrage tricks, including the establishment of a subsidiary in Ireland:

> That subsidiary, Apple Operations International, has no employees and no physical presence, but keeps its bank accounts and records in the United States and holds its board meetings in California. It was incorporated in Ireland in 1980, and is owned and controlled by the US parent company, Apple Inc. . . . Exploiting the gap between the two nations' tax laws, Apple Operations International has not filed an income tax return in either country, or any other country, for the past five years. From 2009 to 2012, it reported income totaling $30 billion.[21]

When Ireland changed its tax laws in 2015, Apple responded by secretly shifting some of its subsidiaries to another international tax haven, the Isle of Jersey.[22]

Adam Smith would not have been surprised. In *The Wealth of Nations* he wrote: "The proprietor of stock is properly a citizen of the world, and is not necessarily attached to any particular country. He would be apt to abandon the country in which he was exposed to a vexatious inquisition, in order to be assessed to a burdensome tax, and would remove his stock to some other country where he could carry on his

business, or enjoy his fortune more at his ease."[23] Nor would
Smith have been surprised by the centrality of labor arbitrage in the modern global economy:

> Our merchants and master manufacturers complain
> much of the bad effects of high wages in raising the
> price, and thereby lessening the sale of their goods
> both at home and abroad. They say nothing concerning the bad effects of high profits. They are silent with
> regard to the pernicious effects of their own gains.
> They complain only of those of other people.[24]

IMMIGRATION ALONG WITH offshoring can be used as a
form of global labor arbitrage. Instead of bringing jobs to
low-wage workers abroad, employers can encourage the importation of low-wage workers to their home countries to
suppress wages, deter unionization, and weaken the bargaining power of native and immigrant workers alike.

Some Western countries have had formal policies of encouraging unskilled, low-wage immigration, like the US
with its exploitative guest worker programs in agriculture
and West Germany with its Turkish *Gastarbeiter* (guest workers). But for the most part, unskilled immigration has been
the incidental result of other policies. In the United States,
most legal unskilled immigrants have been low-income
Mexicans and Central Americans who come on the basis of
US family reunification laws, in addition to 12 million or so
illegal immigrants, mostly from the same nearby countries.
In Europe, asylum laws and refugee policies are the chief

source of unskilled immigration. And some European countries have privileged immigration from former colonies. Whatever the particular regime, in every Western country the low-skilled immigration issue tends to pit the managerial elite against substantial elements of the working-class, native majority.

I N GOVERNMENT, THE result of the half-century neoliberal revolution from above has been to weaken two institutions that amplified the political power of the mid-twentieth-century working class—mass-membership political parties and legislatures.

"The age of party democracy has passed," Peter Mair wrote in *Ruling the Void: The Hollowing of Western Democracy* (2013). "Although the parties remain, they have become so disconnected from the wider society, and pursue a form of competition that is so lacking in meaning, that they no longer seem capable of sustaining democracy in its present form."[25] What were once national federations of local parties with mass membership in many countries have become little more than brand labels used by small groups of politicians, donors, and campaign strategists.

In the United States, the McGovern-Fraser Commission reforms of 1971 sought to democratize the structure of the Democratic Party by replacing nominating conventions dominated by state and local power brokers with citizen primaries. These reforms shifted power from the old white working-class base of the New Deal Democrats to a new Democratic elite, which, while more racially diverse, for the most part was still largely white but far more affluent, educated, culturally liberal, and skeptical of government intervention in markets. On both sides of the Atlantic, the crumbling of mass party federations has created a new politics centered on candidates who are self-funded or adept at raising money or are mass-media celebrities like Arnold Schwarzenegger, Jesse Ventura, Donald Trump, and Beppe Grillo.

In Europe, the erosion of national democracy has been accelerated by the conversion of the European Common Market, a loose trading bloc, into the European Union (EU), a pseudofederal state with its own parliament and its own court and its own executive, the European Commission. Tripartite arrangements among business, labor, and government have not been replicated at the supranational level.[26] The EU displays a chronic bias in favor of business and finance and against organized labor, reflecting the greater ability of investors and corporate managers to lobby and organize across national boundaries. In countries like Italy and Greece, EU bureaucrats allied with bankers and other elite economic groups have several times insisted on governments headed by probusiness technocrats and have dictated promarket reforms reflecting the interests of foreign investors as a condition of aid.[27]

Meanwhile, in both Europe and the US, judiciaries insulated from voters have usurped much of the former authority of legislatures. The US Supreme Court, whose prestige had been enhanced by its interventions in the post-1945 civil rights revolution, has set itself up as an unelected superlegislature, decreeing that policies in one area after another, from regulation of abortion and marriage to campaign finance regulation, belong in the realm of inviolable constitutional rights and must be determined by life-tenured, unelected federal judges, rather than democratic legislatures or citizen initiatives.[28]

The transfer of power from democratic legislatures to courts has not been limited to the United States. "Over the past few years the world has witnessed an astonishingly rapid transition to what may be called *juristocracy*," Ran Hirschl wrote in 2004, explaining: "Conflicts involving contentious political issues are treated as primarily legal questions rather than political ones, with the concomitant assumption that national high courts, instead of elected representatives, should resolve them." Hirschl argues that the major motivation for juristocracy is to shield elites from democratic majorities, by means of "a strategic tripartite pact between hegemonic, yet increasingly threatened, political elites seeking to insulate their policy preferences from the vicissitudes of democratic politics; economic elites who share a commitment to free markets and a concomitant antipathy to government; and supreme courts working to enhance their symbolic power and institutional position."[29]

Counter-majoritarian, rights-based liberalism, pushed too far, becomes antidemocratic liberalism. Many of the institutions important to citizens in democracies are subtly altered or delegitimated in a society in which communal interests must be justified exclusively in terms of this or that individual right. Churches and clubs and families, to name three examples, are impossible to justify on the basis of contracts among rights-bearing individuals, as though they were mere business partnerships. So are institutions like labor unions that magnify working-class power by existing in a third realm of collective bargaining between individual rights and majority rule and can function only if membership is more or less compulsory. It is also difficult for a rights-based philosophy to legitimize the nation-state as a community that can demand loyalty and sacrifice from its members.

Reliance on courts instead of legislatures to shape public policy has shifted power from working-class voters to overclass judges. In the US, appointees to the Supreme Court and the federal judiciary tend to have the most elite social and educational backgrounds of any group in government. They often share the combination of social liberalism and free market economic conservatism that is common in the college-educated Western overclass but unpopular among most voters. The same US federal judiciary that has struck down restrictions on abortion and in favor of gay rights has also consistently ruled against labor unions and struck down legislated limits on allowable political donations by corporations and rich individuals.

Long-overdue victories ending unjust discrimination on the basis of race, sex, and sexual orientation could have been achieved by electoral coalitions to enact democratic legislation, without the imposition by elite judges of libertarian preferences in all spheres of public policy. Government by judiciary tends to be a dictatorship of overclass libertarians in robes.

IN THE REALMS of civil society and culture, an elite-driven revolution from above has occurred as well as in the realms of the economy and government. Secularization and declining church attendance have decimated the ability of denominational institutions to represent the interests and values of working-class believers.

Scholars like Robert D. Putnam have documented the collapse of the once-flourishing network of American mass-membership civic federations like United Way and the American Legion.[30] Overall, the shift of the center of gravity from local chapter-based membership associations and church congregations to foundations, foundation-funded nonprofits, and universities represents a transfer of civic and cultural influence away from ordinary people upward to the managerial elite. Many of today's so-called community organizations are not so much grass roots as AstroTurf (an artificial grass). A contemporary "community activist" is likely to be a university graduate and likely as well to be rich or supported by affluent overclass parents, because of the reliance of nonprofits on unpaid interns and staffers with low salaries. Success in the nonprofit sector frequently depends not on mobilizing ordinary citizens but on getting grants from the program officers of a small number of billionaire-endowed foundations in a few big cities, many of them named for old or new business tycoons, like Ford, Rockefeller, Gates, and Bloomberg. Such "community activists" have more in common with nineteenth-century missionaries sent out to save the "natives" from themselves than with the members of local communities who headed local chapters of national volunteer federations in the past.

The social scientists Theda Skocpol, Rachael V. Cobb, and Cascy Andrew Klofstad have documented an important cause of the decline of civic groups—the withdrawal of political elites from membership in cross-class organizations, in favor of working for nonprofit organizations or joining nonprofit boards whose staffs and members tend to belong to the college-educated overclass. In the words of Skocpol, Cobb, and Klofstad, "American elites . . . went from joining membership associations *along with* fellow citizens from many walks of life, toward joining boards and coordinating committees that left them in the position of doing public-spirited things *for* or *to* ordinary citizens (emphasis in the original)."[31]

IN 2006 THE billionaire Warren Buffett told the commentator Ben Stein, "There's class warfare, all right, but it's my class, the rich class, that's making war, and we're winning."[32]

The triumph of technocratic neoliberalism over democratic pluralism is not the work of a conspiracy or a cabal. The libertarian economist James Buchanan did not meet with the Beat poet Allen Ginsberg halfway between Mont-Pèlerin and Haight-Ashbury in the 1960s to plot a transfer of power in all three realms of politics, economics, and culture from working-class majorities to the university-credentialed overclass in the US and other Western nations.

But the effect of many simultaneous campaigns, each led, staffed, and bankrolled by college-educated overclass reformers, each trying to demolish one wing of the building, was to bring down the whole structure of the post-1945 cross-class settlement in the US and similar Western democracies. When the dust from the collapse cleared, the major institutions in which working-class people had found a voice on the basis of numbers—mass-membership parties, legislatures, trade unions, and grassroots religious and civic institutions—had been weakened or destroyed, leaving most of the nonelite population in Western countries with no voice in public affairs at all, except for shrieks of rage.

CHAPTER FIVE

The Populist Counterrevolution from Below

WHEN A DESTRUCTIVE forest fire breaks out, the question "How did it start?" has two answers. One has to do with what literally started the fire—a spark from a lightning strike, a poorly tended campfire, or the gasoline can of an arsonist. The other answer identifies the reason why dead wood and other tinder was allowed to accumulate over a long period of time in quantities sufficient to enable a single flame to ignite a conflagration.

In the same way, in understanding the populist eruptions that are burning down long-established party systems in Europe and North America, we must distinguish the sparks from the fuel. In different countries the sparks have been different—in Germany a sudden and controversial influx of Middle Eastern immigrants beginning in 2015, in France a regressive tax that fell heavily on working-class citizens, in the United States the migration of millions of illegal immigrants and the devastation of industrial regions by East Asian imports and the decisions of US companies to shutter their factories and replace them with new ones abroad.

But what fuels the conflagration, once kindled, is a mass of grievances that have accumulated over years or decades. The class conflict in the transatlantic West has erupted into a roaring conflagration only recently, with the Brexit vote and the election of Donald Trump in 2016, the coming to power of a coalition of populist outsiders in Italy, the yellow vest protests in France, and other political fires. But the class war has been smoldering for half a century.

For the last two generations, in different decades, and in different Western countries, the occasions of populist protest have been different—the white backlash against the civil rights revolution of the 1960s, the traditionalist backlash against the sexual and censorship revolution of the 1970s, populist resistance to the Japanese import shocks of the 1980s, and then, more recently, mass immigration, globalization, deindustrialization, and the Great Recession. All of these different issues resulted in similar alignments of large portions of the non-college-educated working class against managerial and professional elites.

Long before Brexit and Trump, their lack of voice and influence made alienated native working-class voters—mostly but not exclusively white—a destabilizing force in politics. In the United States, "hardhats" and "Middle American radicals" were already identified as a social force as early as the 1960s and 1970s, when the foreign-born population of the US was at its lowest point and immigration was not a major issue. The antecedents of Trumpism can be traced to a series of independent presidential campaigns that drew many members of the

white working class out of the midcentury New Deal coalition: George Wallace's independent presidential campaign in
1968, which won Wallace 13.5 percent of the popular vote,
and the 1992 campaign of Ross Perot, who captured 19 percent, the highest percentage for a third-party candidate since
Theodore Roosevelt ran as the candidate of the Progressive
Party in 1912. Although he was a Texan, Perot did poorly
among white southerners and did best among high-school-
educated whites in the industrial North. In 2000 Donald
Trump considered running for president as the candidate of
Perot's short-lived Reform Party.

In Europe as well, populist nationalism was part of the
political landscape long before its dramatic breakthroughs in
the second decade of the twenty-first century. In 2002, disaffected former mainstream party voters in addition to the
tiny number of far-right voters permitted the anti-Semitic
neofascist candidate Jean-Marie Le Pen to make it to the second round in the French presidential elections. The only reason there was a British referendum on membership in the
European Union at all was the desire of British conservatives
to appease a growing number of populist voters. Before the
British "Leave" vote won the Brexit referendum in 2016,
Dutch and French voters in 2005 and Irish voters in 2008
had rejected measures promoting greater centralization of
the European Union in referendums. In all three countries,
political elites later succeeded in maneuvers to ensure that
the popular referendum results were nullified.

As a political phenomenon, then, populism in the West is
nothing new. It is an ongoing counterrevolution from below
against the half-century-long technocratic neoliberal revolution

from above imposed by Western managerial elites. At every stage, populist movements of some sort have resisted technocratic neoliberalism. Again and again, because of their lack of wealth, power, and cultural influence, the populists have lost, becoming more alienated and more resentful. And so the dry wood accumulates to fuel the next conflagration.

THANKS TO THE neoliberal revolution from above since the 1960s, on both sides of the Atlantic there are substantial numbers of voters—by no means only white or only working class—who have a coherent mix of public policy preferences that are ignored by national politicians and policy makers. These voters combine support for generous government entitlement like public pensions and health care spending with opposition to high levels of unskilled immigration and moderate cultural conservatism—what the British political scientist Matthew Goodwin calls a combination of economic and cultural protection.[1]

How big is this populist group? In 2015, the political scientist Lee Drutman, then my colleague at New America, the think tank I cofounded, used survey data to map voters on two axes—one involving attitudes toward immigration and one involving attitudes toward Social Security. The diagram that resulted has since achieved considerable fame in the small world of social science charts.

Drutman calculated that in the United States, "populists"—defined as those who favored maintaining or increasing Social Security spending, while maintaining or decreasing immigration—made up 40.3 percent of the electorate, while "moderate leftists" (American "liberals" or "progressives"), who supported maintaining or increasing both Social Security and immigration, made up 32.9 percent, with "moderates" (who wanted no changes in either Social Security or immigration) at 20.5 percent. The two groups that wanted to cut Social Security and increase immigration, "business conservatives" (3.8 percent), who are better described as "neoliberals," and "political conservatives" (2.4 percent), who might also be described as "libertarians," made up only 6.2 percent of voters.

In light of the fact that populists in the US, defined by this measure, outnumber neoliberals and libertarians combined by more than six to one in the American electorate, why is it that no party—indeed, no wing of either of the two major parties—represents their views? Drutman speculates that neoliberalism is the view of "the wealthy donors who are eager to cut entitlements because they are worried about high taxes and are also eager to expand immigration because they'd like to have more potential employees to choose from." According to Drutman, both populists and "business Republicans" tend to support the Republican Party. The business Republicans, whose preferences Republican politicians promote, on average make $69,711 a year, around $30,000 more than the Republican populists, whose preferences most Republican politicians ignore.[2]

The second-largest group of voters in the American electorate, those whom Drutman calls "liberals," that is, the moderate left, shares liberal cultural views and support of mass immigration with the free market libertarian right. But on economic policy issues, leftists, agreeing with populists on issues like Social Security spending, find their policy preferences neglected by the much smaller but more influential neoliberal faction of the Democratic Party.

One way to understand these results is to recognize that in the United States and similar Western democracies there are two political spectrums, one for the college-educated managerial-professional overclass minority and one for the non-college-educated working-class majority of all races. Each of these class-based political spectrums has its own "right," its own "left," and its own "center."

The overclass political spectrum is bounded on the right by extreme free market libertarianism of the kind associated with the economist Milton Friedman and promoted by the Koch brothers and the Cato Institute in the US. The elite political spectrum is bounded on the left by moderate, market-friendly neoliberalism of the kind associated with the Clintons and Obama in the US, Blair and Brown in the UK, and Schröder in Germany. The center of the elite political spectrum is occupied by moderate business-class conservatives like the Bush dynasty in the US, former prime ministers David Cameron and Theresa May in the UK, Angela Merkel and the Christian Democrats in Germany, and Emmanuel Macron and his supporters in France.

The "left," "right," and "center" of the working-class political spectrum are quite different from the equivalent positions on the overclass political spectrum. The leftmost point on the spectrum combines leftist cultural attitudes with something like old-fashioned European social democracy, supportive of government aid to citizens and socially liberal. The rightmost point is defined by conservative populism—socially conservative on issues of sex and reproduction, but supportive of government programs that help the working class, like Medicare and Social Security in the US. The "center" can be identified with what the sociologist Donald Warren in the 1970s called "Middle American Radicalism"—moderate social attitudes combined with prolabor, New Deal–style democratic pluralism.

To put it another way, the center of gravity of the overclass is center-right (promarket) on economic issues and center-left (antitraditional) on social issues. In comparison, the center of gravity of the much larger working class is center-left on economic issues and center-right on social issues.

Populists combined with social democratic leftists make up half or more of the US population, but they are almost completely unrepresented among the college-educated overclass professionals who make up most of the personnel in legislatures, executive agencies, courts, corporate suites, think tanks, universities, philanthropies, and media corporations. This explains why, for the last generation, "centrism" in American politics has been defined as overclass centrism, identified with support for cutting working-class entitlements like Social Security and Medicare in the name of "fiscal responsibility," while embracing individualistic liberal views of reproduction and sex and, more recently, gender identity. Meanwhile, the "radical center," the midpoint of the working-class majority's political spectrum, has either been ignored by politicians and pundits and academics altogether or grossly mischaracterized by overclass journalists and overclass academics as the "far right" and lumped together with neo-Nazis and the Ku Klux Klan.

T HE SINGLE MOST important factor explaining the rise of
populism in the US and Western Europe is the changing class composition of center-left parties between the mid-
twentieth century and the early twenty-first. What used to
be parties of the native white working class and rural voters
have become parties of upscale members of the native white
managerial elite, allied with racial and ethnic minorities and
immigrants. Following the 2018 midterm elections, forty-
two of the wealthiest fifty congressional districts in the
United States were represented by Democrats.[3] Between
2010 and 2018, whites with a college degree went from 40
to 29 percent of the voters in the Republican Party, while
white voters with less than a college education expanded
from 50 to 59 percent of the Republican electorate, a trend
that accelerated during the campaign and presidency of
Donald Trump.[4]

The Democratic Party in the US is now a party of the affluent native white metropolitan elite, allied with immigrants
and native minorities brought together by noneconomic
identity politics rather than by class politics. In Britain, the
social base of the Labour Party has undergone a similar shift.
In Germany, the Green Party shares the best-educated and
wealthiest voters of the managerial-professional overclass with
the free market libertarian Free Democrats.[5]

The exclusion of the views of large numbers of voters
from any representation in public policy or debate has created
openings in politics that demagogic populists have sought to
fill. Alone among Republican candidates in the 2016 presi-

dential primaries, Donald Trump both denounced the Iraq War as a mistake and opposed cuts to Social Security and Medicare. This combination of views was the exact opposite of the orthodox conservative party line. George W. Bush, after all, had invaded Iraq and had sought to cut Social Security by means of partial privatization. Indeed, Trump's stance on Social Security put him to the left of then-president Barack Obama, who, like Bush, had proposed cutting Social Security, by the different method of altering how it is indexed for inflation. Trump's positions were heretical in the Republican Party and the American establishment as a whole. But they were popular with millions of American voters. And so Trump went on to defeat George W. Bush's brother and would-be successor, Jeb Bush, in the Republican primaries, and then to defeat Hillary Clinton in the electoral college, in part by appealing to former Democratic voters in the Midwest whom neoliberal overclass Democrats had ignored.

Where populists have succeeded in Western countries, they have done so because they have opportunistically championed legitimate positions that are shared by many voters but excluded from the narrow neoliberal overclass political spectrum. In particular, they have given voice to popular concerns about trade and immigration that have been ignored for decades by the managerial ruling class.

In the late twentieth century, when its electoral base was still the native-born working class, the Democratic Party was more favorable to protectionist trade policies and restrictionist immigration policies than the Republicans, then the party of the employer elite. Thanks in part to the trade issue, many former working-class whites have migrated into the Republican Party in the last few decades, while elite white college-educated professionals and their children increasingly have favored the Democrats. As a result of the changing class composition of the two parties, the older dichotomy of Democratic protectionism and Republican support for free trade has been reversed. According to the Pew Research Center, by a margin of 56 percent to 38 percent, Democratic voters believe that free trade agreements have been good for the US. Among Republicans, those numbers are flipped: by a 53 percent to 38 percent margin, a majority of Republicans believe free trade has been a bad thing. While partisan affiliations have changed over time, the underlying division over globalization among overclass voters and working-class voters has not.

In immigration policy as in trade policy, the mainstream parties in the US and Europe have reversed positions, reflecting their changing class makeup. The historian of organized labor Vernon Briggs observed that "it is not surprising that at every juncture and with no exception prior to the 1990s, the American labor movement either directly instigated or strongly endorsed every legislative initiative by the US Congress to regulate and to restrict immigration. It also supported all related efforts to strengthen enforcement of these policies."[6]

In the 1990s the US Commission on Immigration Reform was appointed by President Bill Clinton, at a time when the Democratic Party was still influenced in part by the historic skepticism of organized labor toward large-scale immigration. While denouncing bigotry against immigrants, the commission called for reducing legal immigration, shifting the basis of immigration away from family relationships toward skills, and promoting the integration of immigrants.[7] In the words of the chair of the commission, Barbara Jordan, the first African American woman from the South to be elected to Congress, "The commission finds no national interest in continuing to import lesser skilled and unskilled workers to compete in the most vulnerable parts of our labor force."[8] Jordan also rejected efforts to blur the distinction between legal and illegal immigration: "To make sense about the national interest in immigration, it is necessary to make distinctions between those who obey the law, and those who violate it. Therefore, we disagree, also, with those who label our efforts to control illegal immigration as somehow inherently anti-immigrant. Unlawful immigration is unacceptable."[9] A generation later, most of the policies proposed by the Jordan Commission are supported by the populist Republican right and denounced by growing numbers of self-described "progressive" Democrats for whom any enforcement of immigration laws is inherently unjust.

The startling adoption by the American center-left since the 1990s of support for high levels of unskilled immigration, a position historically associated with right-wing libertarians and business lobbies, is partly opportunistic, based on the hope that immigrant voters and their descendants can make possible permanent one-party Democratic control of the US government. And it is partly a reaction to nativism by conservatives who mischaracterize Latino immigrants as criminals and "invaders." But the center-left reversal on immigration policy also reflects the historic shift in the Democratic Party's white voters from working-class whites to affluent, university-educated members of the white overclass and business and finance. At the turn of the twenty-first century, the severely shrunken private labor movement, while maintaining its skepticism about free trade, gave up its historic public opposition to high levels of legal and illegal immigration as the price of continuing membership in the transformed, more employer-friendly Democratic coalition.[10]

Notwithstanding business-financed propaganda about the alleged need for higher immigration of all kinds, proposals to increase numerical levels of immigration remain profoundly unpopular in Western democracies, even among voters who are well-disposed to individual immigrants and immigration in general. In a 2018 Pew Research Center poll of twenty-seven countries that take half of the world's immigrants, including the US, Canada, and Western European nations, a median of 45 percent wanted fewer or no immigrants and 36 percent were satisfied with the existing number. Only 14 percent thought their countries should allow more immigrants. In the US in 2018, a mere 24 percent wanted to admit greater numbers of immigrants each year, while 73 percent wanted the same number (44 percent) or fewer to none (29 percent). In Germany, where Chancellor Angela Merkel allowed a large influx of Syrian and other refugees in 2015, 58 percent wanted fewer or no immigrants and only 19 percent wanted a higher level of immigration. In both Britain and France, only 16 percent favored raising the level of immigration.[11]

A Harvard CAPS/Harris Poll in 2018 found that 64 percent of Americans, including 53 percent of Latinos, favor immediately deporting anyone who crosses the border illegally;

70 percent support more restrictive immigration laws.[12] If, as many overclass neoliberals claim, supporting enforcement of immigration laws is motivated solely by "white nationalism," then overwhelming numbers of Americans, including a majority of Latinos, must be "white nationalists."

I N CARRYING OUT their counterrevolution from outside and below, today's populist demagogues target their overclass establishment enemies in all three realms of social power: politics, the economy, and the culture.

In politics, today's populists champion majoritarian democracy against decision-making by the unelected, technocratic bodies to which much authority has been transferred during the recent neoliberal revolution. In Europe, this means "Euroskepticism" and "sovereigntism," the assertion of the sovereignty of the democratic nation-state and the democratic national legislature against the power of the transnational bureaucracies of the European Union. In the United States, the equivalent is the Trump administration's transactional approach to treaties and international organizations, which tend to be venerated by technocratic neoliberals as pillars of a "liberal world order."

In the economy, today's populist leaders tend to be economic nationalists, opposing global labor arbitrage policies of offshoring and mass immigration, which the overclass establishment claims are both inevitable and beneficial. Populist constituencies include many workers in manufacturing districts hit hard by foreign competition, including China's subsidized "social dumping," and others who view immigrants as competitors for jobs, public services, or status.

In the culture, populist politicians deliberately flout the elaborate etiquette of overclass corporations and universities by using crude and belligerent language. They mock "political correctness," the artificial dialect devised by leftist activists and spread by university and corporate bureaucrats that serves as a class marker distinguishing the college-educated from the vulgar majority below them.

At its worst, the majoritarianism of Western populists blurs into what the sociologist Pierre van den Berghe calls "*Herrenvolk* democracy," the identification of "the nation" or "the people" with the numerically largest racial or religious community in a nation-state. Donald Trump's defiant use of "Merry Christmas" instead of the more inclusive "Happy Holidays" and Italian interior minister Matteo Salvini's order that public buildings in Italy display Catholic crucifixes are examples of *Herrenvolk* populism with a religious tinge. Trump's contemptuous references to the ancestral countries of non-white American political opponents and his description of African nations as "shithole countries" are blatantly racist. Such rhetoric, and the fact that some parties with fascist roots like Marine Le Pen's National Front and the Sweden Democrats have succeeded in tapping into populist discontent, has made it easy for defenders of the embattled neoliberal establishment to dismiss all populist voters as white supremacists.

But equating most populist voters with far-right extremists is as absurd as efforts by right-wingers to lump center-left neoliberals and social democrats together with communists. Only a tiny number of Europeans or Americans are white supremacist radicals who dream of racially pure "ethnostates" or anti-Semites who believe that immigration is a part of a global Jewish conspiracy to "replace" Western nations. Many populist voters until recently voted for prolabor, center-left parties like the Democrats in the US, Labour in the UK, and the Social Democrats in Germany, before "leftism" and "progressivism" were redefined to mean a combination of open-borders globalism, antinationalism, and radical race- and gender-based identity politics. For example, in Britain, in the 2019 elections for the European Parliament, an estimated 14 percent of voters who supported Labour in 2017 defected to vote for Nigel Farage's new Brexit Party. It is more plausible to assume that they did so out of concerns about national and popular sovereignty than to believe that before 2019 one in seven Labour voters was a cryptofascist white supremacist.[13]

The actual antecedents of contemporary populist politicians like Trump are to be found not in interwar Central European totalitarian states but in state and local politics, particularly urban politics. In Europe, pro-Brexit Boris Johnson was the mayor of London before becoming prime minister, and Italy's Matteo Salvini was on the city council of Milan from 1993 to 2012.

In the United States, the shift from post-1945 democratic pluralism to technocratic neoliberalism was fostered from the 1960s onward by an alliance of the white overclass with African Americans and other racial minority groups. The result was a backlash by white working-class voters, not only against nonwhites who were seen as competitors for jobs and housing, but also against the alien cultural liberalism of white "gentry liberals." The backlash in the North was particularly intense among "white ethnics"—first-, second-, and third-generation white immigrants like Irish, German, Italian, and Polish

Americans, many of them Catholic. The disproportionately working-class white ethnics now found themselves defined as bigots by the same white Anglo-Saxon Protestant (WASP) elites who until recently had imposed quotas on Jews and Catholics in their Ivy League universities, but who were now posing as the virtuous, enlightened champions of civil rights.

This toxic mix of black aspiration, white ethnic backlash, and WASP condescension provided a ripe habitat for demagogues, many of them old-school Democrats like Frank Rizzo, mayor of Philadelphia, Sam Yorty, mayor of Los Angeles, and Mario Angelo Procaccino, failed mayoral candidate in New York. These populist big-city mayors or candidates in the second half of the twentieth century combined appeals to working-class grievances and resentments with folksy language and feuds with the metropolitan press, a pattern practiced, in different ways, by later New York City mayors Ed Koch, a Democrat, and Rudy Giuliani, a Republican.

In its "Against Trump" issue of January 22, 2016, the editors of *National Review* mocked the "funky outer-borough accents" shared by Donald Trump and Bernie Sanders.[14] Indeed, Trump, a "white ethnic" from Queens with German and Scots ancestors, with his support in the US industrial states where working-class non-British European-Americans are concentrated, is ethnically different from most of his predecessors in the White House, whose ancestors were proportionately far more British American. Traits which seem outlandish in a US president would not have seemed so if Trump had been elected mayor of New York. Donald Trump was not Der Führer. He was Da Mayor of America.

THE WEAKNESS OF populism is that it is literally reactionary. Populists react against what the dominant overclass establishment does, rather than having a positive and constructive agenda of their own.

Today's populism is a counterculture, not a counterestablishment. A counterculture defines itself in opposition to the establishment. A counterestablishment wants to be the establishment. Members of a counterculture relish their outsider status. Members of a counterestablishment regret their outsider status. A counterculture is the heckler in the audience. A counterestablishment is the understudy, waiting in the wings for a chance to play the title role.

Populists are better at campaigning than at governing, as President-Elect Trump discovered when he found it difficult to staff his administration with competent technocrats willing to serve under a politician despised by many experts and officials. Demagogues are good at channeling popular grievances and bad at redressing them. Populist movements that deride expertise and bureaucracy naturally tend to have few experts of their own to formulate policies and administer agencies. The vacuum of experienced talent is often filled by cronies or relatives of the populist demagogue.

Populist demagogues cannot even be truly representative. No single charismatic individual or party can substitute for institutionalized representation of a pluralistic society in all its variety in all three spheres of politics, the economy, and the culture.

From the perspective of democratic pluralism, technocratic neoliberalism and demagogic populism represent different highways to the hell of autocracy. According to technocratic neoliberalism, an elite of experts insulated from mass prejudice and ignorance can best promote the public interest. According to populism, a single Caesarist or Bonapartist figure with a mystical, personal connection to the masses can represent the people as a whole.

Both minoritarian rule by enlightened technocrats and pseudo-majoritarian rule by charismatic tribunes of the people are rejected by democratic pluralism, based as it is on a vision of society as a complex whole composed of many legitimate communities, each with its own institutions and representatives, rather than a fluctuating mass of atomized individuals. In 1999 the British politician and scholar David Marquand wrote:

Pluralists rejoice in variety. They are sceptical about theories—Marxism, economic liberalism, globalisation—that presuppose uniformity. Pluralists like the clash and clang of argument; the monochrome sameness of the big battalions horrifies them; so does the sugary conformism of the politically correct. Instinctively, they are for the "little platoons" that Edmund Burke saw as the nurseries of "public affections," and they want to protect them from the homogenising pressures of state, market and opinion. For them, a good society is a mosaic of vibrant smaller collectivities—trade unions, universities, business associations, local authorities, miners' welfares, churches, mosques, Women's Institutes, NGOs—each with its own identity, tradition, values and rituals. Thomas Hobbes, the philosopher of absolute sovereignty, famously compared such collectivities to "worms in the entrails of a natural man." Pluralists see them as antibodies protecting the culture of democracy from infection.[15]

Half a century earlier in 1953, the American thinker Robert Nisbet made a similar argument:

[T]he role of political government becomes clear in the democracies. Not to sterilize the normal authorities of associations, as does the total State through a pre-emption of function, deprivation of authority, and a monopolization of allegiance, but to reinforce these associations, to provide, administratively, a means whereby the normal competition of group differences is held in bounds and an environment of law in which no single authority, religious or economic, shall attain a repressive and monopolistic influence—this is the role of government in a democracy.[16]

Genuine democracy requires never-ending, institutionalized negotiations among many major social groups in politics, the economy, and the culture, each equipped with substantial bargaining power and the ability to defend its interests and values. By this definition, technocratic neoliberalism and demagogic populism are not forms of democracy at all.

THE HISTORICAL RECORD in many countries shows that when populist outsiders challenge oligarchic insiders, the oligarchs almost always win. The oligarchs may not have numbers, but they control most of the wealth, expertise, and political influence and dominate the media, universities, and nonprofit sectors. Most populist waves break and disperse on the concrete seawalls of elite privilege.

Oscillation among oligarchy and populism has long been the dynamic in much of Latin America.[17] In the American South in the century between the Civil War and the civil rights revolution, when politics was contested by oligarchs and demagogues, most populist politicians gave up or sold out. In some cases, like that of Texas governor and US senator W. Lee "Pappy" O'Daniel, a country music singer, they were simply folksy fronts for corporate and upper-class interests all along.

The few populists in the American South who maintained some independence were those who could finance themselves, usually by corrupt means. Louisiana governor Huey Long could battle the ruling families and the powerful corporations because he skimmed money from state employee checks and kept it in a locked "deduct box."[18] In Texas, anti-Klan populist governor James "Pa" Ferguson, along with his wife, Miriam "Ma" Ferguson, who, following the impeachment of her husband, was elected governor on the slogan "Two Governors for the Price of One," sold pardons to the relatives of convicted criminals.[19] As billionaires who could finance their own campaigns, Ross Perot and Donald Trump could claim to be free to run against the American establishment.

The rise of charismatic populist tribunes as a response to the increasing social and epistemic closure of Western elites was entirely to be expected. Now that access to political influence depends not on decentralized grassroots party organizations and farm associations and unions and civic and church federations but on donations from billionaires or personal media celebrity, it is only natural that working-class outsiders will turn to champions who are rich business executives like Ross Perot, TV celebrities like Italy's Beppe Grillo, or a combination of both, like billionaire and reality television star Donald Trump or media tycoon Silvio Berlusconi. Absent advocates like these, many disconnected voters would have little or no voice at all.

For their part, would-be tribunes of the people like Trump, Farage, Berlusconi, and Salvini benefit from the wrath of the establishments that condemn them. The more they are denounced, the more plausible is their claim that, despite their celebrity or riches, they too are outsiders despised by the insiders, just like their nonelite constituents.

Populism is a symptom of a sick body politic, not a cure. In a formally democratic oligarchy, a nepotistic elite runs things for the benefit of its members most of the time. On the rare occasions when a demagogue is elected to office, he or she will be less likely to reform the system than to join the establishment or build a corrupt personal political machine, steering government patronage to supporters.

Those who favor democracy can look on this kind of

political order only with dismay. Formal democracy may survive, but its spirit has fled. No matter who wins, the insiders or outsiders, the majority will lose. When a society is trapped in a vicious circle in which selfish oligarchs alternate with populist hucksters, economic growth and the rule of law are all likely to be casualties.

Is this the future of the West—never-ending clashes between North Atlantic versions of Juan Perón and the equivalent of the Buenos Aires Jockey Club? This is not as grim a fate as the breakdown of the Weimar Republic in Germany followed by the rise of National Socialism. But a world of decaying democracies dominated by oligarchic factions, in which alienated mobs now and then use elections as an excuse to demonstrate inchoate rage, is dystopian enough.

CHAPTER SIX

Russian Puppets and Nazis: How the Managerial Elite Demonizes Populist Voters

THE POPULIST WAVE IN politics on both sides of the Atlantic is a defensive reaction against the technocratic neoliberal revolution from above that has been carried out in the last half century by national managerial elites. Over the last half century, the weakening or destruction by neoliberal policy makers of the intermediary institutions of mid-twentieth century democratic pluralism, particularly labor unions, has deprived much of the working class of effective voice or agency in government, the economy, and culture. Populist demagogues can channel the legitimate grievances of many working-class voters, but they cannot create a stable, institutionalized alternative to overclass-dominated neoliberalism. Only a new democratic pluralism that compels managerial elites to share power with the multiracial, religiously pluralistic working class in the economy, politics, and the culture can end the cycle of oscillation between oppressive technocracy and destructive populism.

That is the thesis of this book. It is a minority viewpoint within overclass circles in the US and Europe. A far more common view among transatlantic elites interprets the success of populist and nationalist candidates in today's Western democracies not as a predictable and disruptive backlash against oligarchic misrule, but as a revival of Nazi or Soviet-style totalitarianism. One narrative holds that Russian president Vladimir Putin's regime, by cleverly manipulating public opinion in the West through selective leaks to the media or Internet advertisements and memes, is responsible for Brexit, the election of Trump in 2016, and perhaps other major political events. A rival narrative sees no need to invoke Russian machinations; in this view, without aid from abroad, demagogues can trigger the latent "authoritarian personalities" of voters, particularly white working-class native voters, many of whom, it is claimed, will turn overnight into a fascist army if properly mobilized. These two elite narratives, promulgated by antipopulist politicians, journalists, and academics, can be called the Russia Scare and the Brown Scare (after earlier "brown scares" in Western democracies, with the color referring to Hitler's Brownshirts).[1]

The reductio ad absurdum of this kind of mythological thinking is the adoption of the term "Resistance" by domestic opponents of President Donald Trump, which implies an equation between Democrats and anti-Trump Republicans and the heroic anti-Nazis of the French Resistance. The antifascist theme also provides the name for the Antifa movement which, like the earlier "black bloc" anarchist movement, is made up chiefly of the privileged children of the white overclass who abuse leftist ideology as an excuse to dress up as movie-style ninjas, vandalize property, and harass people.[2]

It is no doubt emotionally satisfying for members of the embattled managerial overclass to identify antiestablishment populism with pro-Russian treason, fascism, or both. But this kind of paranoid demonological thinking has the potential to be a greater danger to liberal democracy in the West than any particular populist movements.

To begin with, both the Russia Scare and the Brown Scare betray a profound contempt on the part of members of technocratic neoliberal national establishments for voters who support populist causes or candidates. These voters are assumed to be gullible dimwits who are easily manipulated by foreign propaganda or domestic demagogues. Even worse, attributing populism to the irrational impulses of maladjusted voters prevents embattled establishments on both sides of the Atlantic from treating specific grievances of those voters as legitimate.

Worst of all, the myth that Russia swung the 2016 US presidential election from Clinton to Trump, and endlessly repeated comparisons of current events to the rise of the Nazis in Germany's Weimar Republic, provide the managerial overclasses in Atlantic democracies with excuses to increase their near-monopoly of political, economic, and media power by freezing out political challengers and censoring dissident media. If most opponents of neoliberalism are Russian pawns or potential Nazis, then mere disagreement with neoliberal policies on trade, immigration, taxation, or other subjects can be equated with rejection of liberalism or democracy, if not outright treason. Confronted with peaceful challenges via the voting booth to neoliberal orthodoxy from outsiders on both the populist right and the socialist left, the instinctive reflex of many in the besieged establishment is to call for censorship and repression.

I N THE 1950s, McCarthyism on the right took the form of conservatives accusing establishment liberals of being pawns of Soviet Russia. Today, a new McCarthyism of the center takes the form of establishment neoliberals accusing populists of being pawns of post-Soviet Russia.

If the Russia Scare version of the establishment's anti-populist story line is to be believed, the government of Russian president Vladimir Putin successfully used Western social media platforms like Facebook, Instagram, and Twitter to hypnotize substantial numbers of citizens of North America and Europe into voting against their natural inclinations for Brexit or Donald Trump or Bernie Sanders in 2016. Even the French yellow vest protests and the gains made by Jeremy Corbyn's Labour Party in the British general election of 2017 have been attributed to Russian machinations online.[3]

The "Russiagate" scandal began before Trump's election as the Clinton campaign, some anti-Trump Republicans, elements in the Obama administration, and various members of the US law enforcement and national security establishments spread rumors of alleged links between Russia and the Trump campaign to the media, including the false story that Trump was being blackmailed by Moscow with a videotape of him consorting with Russian prostitutes. When Trump won, his political enemies in the Democratic and Republican parties claimed that Russia had swung the election against

Clinton. Putin had installed his puppet in the White House, it was widely asserted, by one of two methods (or both). One was Russian assistance to the website WikiLeaks, which leaked material damaging to Clinton and her allies. The other method of Russian interference in the 2016 election took the form of propaganda on Facebook, YouTube, and other social media platforms to suppress black voters and encourage some white voters who had voted for Obama in 2012 to vote for Trump in 2016.

In Spring 2019, after a two-year investigation, Special Counsel Robert Mueller found no evidence that the Trump campaign conspired with Russia to influence the 2016 presidential election, leaving many Americans who had believed that the president would be exposed as a traitor disoriented and depressed.[4] However, Mueller and his team, in addition to indicting some Trump campaign officials on unrelated charges, did charge a number of Russians with criminal interference in the 2016 election, allowing Trump's opponents to salvage the thesis that Clinton would have become president of the United States but for Putin's interference.

Like any effective thriller movie or novel, this narrative seeks to achieve realism by weaving facts into a formulaic conspiracy-based plot. It is a fact that Putin, like many Russians, resents the treatment of Russia by the West after the Cold War, symbolized by the incorporation of former Russian satellites into the European Union and the expansion of NATO. Russian nationalists and many populists in Europe and the US share a common hostility to the transnational European Union as well as contemporary transatlantic social liberalism. In addition, Western intelligence authorities claim that Russian intelligence operatives have engaged in trying to promote conflict in the US and other countries by helping whistle-blowers like WikiLeaks and Edward Snowden leak stolen or classified information and by bombarding carefully targeted audiences with Internet memes and ads.

Let us stipulate that this is all true. It was also true in the 1950s that there really were a small number of communists in the US, including a few high-ranking government officials, who spied for the Soviet Union, as well as many more Soviet sympathizers. There were also genuine Soviet disinformation campaigns in the Cold War West. But only the lunatic fringe of the anticommunist right during the Cold War drew the conclusion that the president was a Soviet agent or that main-stream politicians were secret communists. In contrast, influential members of today's American establishment, not only marginal conspiracy theorists, in order to absolve Hillary Clinton of blame for losing the 2016 election, have promoted the claim that the forty-fifth US president was installed by a foreign government and does its bidding. A Gallup poll in August 2018 showed that 78 percent of Democrats believed not only that Russia interfered in the election but also that it changed the outcome, denying Hillary Clinton the presidency.[5]

It is not enough to demonstrate that Putin hoped that Hillary Clinton would be defeated. Great numbers of Americans hoped that she would be defeated as well. It is necessary therefore to demonstrate that the Internet activity of Russian trolls, rather than purely domestic opposition to her candidacy, was the decisive factor in the outcome of the 2016 presidential election.

In the context of election-year advertising, the quantity

of Russian memes was negligible. According to Facebook, only 1 in 23,000 pieces of content on its platform could be traced to Russian sources. Facebook ads linked to Russia cost $46,000, or 0.05 percent of the $81 million that the Clinton and Trump campaigns themselves spent on Facebook ads.[6]

Is it possible that the Russian memes, although mere drops in the ocean of advertising by the Clinton and Trump campaigns, were disproportionately effective in influencing American voters because of their unique sophistication? One anti-Clinton ad on Facebook attributed to Russian trolls showed a photo of Bernie Sanders with the words: "Bernie Sanders: The Clinton Foundation is a 'Problem.'" A pro-Trump meme, presumably targeting religious conservatives, showed Satan wrestling with Jesus. Satan: "If I win Clinton wins!" Jesus: "Not if I can help it!"[7]

To believe the Russia Scare theory of the 2016 US presidential election, we must believe that the staff of Russia's government-linked Internet Research Agency and other Russian saboteurs understood how to influence the psychology of black American voters and white working-class voters in the Midwest far better than did the Clinton and Trump presidential campaigns. The Russians knew which memes or leaked memos would cause black Democrats to vote in lower numbers for Clinton in 2016 than they had voted for Obama for president in 2008 and 2012 and also knew exactly what material would motivate a significant minority of white working-class Obama voters to vote for Trump. In addition to being very flattering to the intelligence of Russian Internet trolls, this is very condescending to those two groups of voters, to say the least.

As it happens, the US election results can be explained

with no need to posit the ability of the Russian government to alter the outcomes of US elections by brainwashing American voters, even if it sought to do so. In December 2015, the progressive documentary filmmaker Michael Moore told *Business Insider*: "Donald Trump is absolutely going to be the Republican candidate for president of the United States."[8] In July 2016, after Trump won the nomination to become the presidential candidate of the Republican Party, Moore wrote an essay on his website, "5 Reasons Why Trump Will Win."

Russian meme warfare on the Internet was not one of Moore's five reasons. According to Moore, who had achieved fame by documenting the industrial decline of the Midwest, the most important reason why Trump would defeat Clinton was the regional economy:

Midwest Math, or Welcome to Our Rust Belt Brexit. I believe Trump is going to focus much of his attention on the four blue states in the rustbelt of the upper Great Lakes—Michigan, Ohio, Pennsylvania and Wisconsin. Four traditionally Democratic states— but each of them have elected a **Republican** governor since 2010 (only Pennsylvania has now finally elected a Democrat). . . . Trump is going to hammer Clinton on this and her support of TPP and other trade policies that have royally screwed the people of these four states. . . . From Green Bay to Pittsburgh, this, my friends, is the middle of England—broken, depressed, struggling, the smokestacks strewn across the countryside with the carcass of what we use to call the Middle Class. . . . What happened in the UK with Brexit is going to happen here. . . . And this is where the math comes in. In 2012, Mitt Romney lost by 64 electoral votes. Add up the electoral votes cast by Michigan, Ohio, Pennsylvania and Wisconsin. It's 64. All Trump needs to do to win is to carry, as he's expected to do, the swath of traditional red states from Idaho to Georgia (states that'll **never** vote for Hillary Clinton), and then he just needs these four rust belt states. He doesn't need Florida. He doesn't need Colorado or Virginia. Just Michigan, Ohio, Pennsylvania and Wisconsin. And that will put him over the top. This is how it will happen in November.[9]

Moore was not the only observer who pointed out that Trump had a possible path to victory in the electoral college. In February 2016, the progressive political analyst Ruy Teixeira told MSNBC that even if Trump alienated black and Latino voters, he might win by sweeping the upper Midwest: "You could see a situation where someone like Trump could carry Ohio, Iowa, Wisconsin, maybe Pennsylvania."[10] In the event, Trump got a higher share of the black vote and the Latino vote than Romney in 2012.[11]

For what it is worth, on May 24, 2016, at a forum in Los Angeles on "Populism Past and Present" hosted by Ian Masters that featured me and the historian Michael Kazin, I was asked if I thought Trump could win. I replied, "I think it's possible. I wouldn't bet on it." I noted that sometimes "a big chunk of the former electoral college presidential majority migrates to the other party." I said that I doubted there would be a "big enough chunk of people who formerly voted

Democratic moving over to put Trump in the White House" but I hedged my bets by saying, "I may look foolish in November."[12]

The political scientist Alan I. Abramowitz has observed that Trump actually performed less well than might have been expected in 2016 in Michigan, Pennsylvania, and Wisconsin, given shifts already under way from the Democrats to the Republicans in those states: "There is no evidence here that Russian interference, to the extent that it occurred, did anything to help Trump in these three states."[13]

In 2018, Hillary Clinton told Britain's Channel Four News: "The real question is how did the Russians know how to target their messages so precisely to undecided voters in Wisconsin or Michigan or Pennsylvania—that is really the nub of the question."[14] No, the real question is why so much of the US and European establishment accepted and promulgated Clinton's alibi for her failure to follow her husband into the office of president of the United States. A Clinton or a Bush was president, vice president, or secretary of state in every year between 1981 and 2013, an era in which working-class incomes stagnated, offshoring devastated US and European manufacturing, the world suffered the worst economic collapse since the Great Depression of the 1930s, and the US plunged into multiple disastrous wars in the Middle East and Central Asia. Trump became president by running against a Bush in the Republican primaries and a Clinton in the general election. The desire of many American voters to disrupt the quarter-century cycle of nearly identical versions of technocratic neoliberalism under alternating Bushes and Clintons is quite sufficient to explain the presidential election of 2016.

THE RUSSIA SCARE STORY is only one of the two narratives that embattled members of the Western establishment are using to explain the rise of transatlantic populism in a way that demonizes populist voters and politicians. The narrative of the post-2016 Brown Scare might be called the Weimar Republic scenario. In this account, contemporary citizens in Europe and North America who voted for Brexit, Trump, and other populist causes are just like the voters who brought Hitler and his National Socialist Party to power in Germany in 1933.

Good thriller fiction is not necessarily good history. Far from being antiestablishment populists, opposed by most of the college-educated, prosperous elites of their nations, Mussolini and Hitler enjoyed substantial support from military, bureaucratic, and business elites in Italy and Germany who feared the working class and viewed fascism as a bulwark against communism, socialism, and liberal democracy. The myth that fascism was brought to power by less-educated members of the working class is nevertheless useful for managerial elites in Washington, London, Paris, and Berlin as they seek to delegitimate populist challenges to their political, economic, and cultural hegemony.

Former US secretary of state Madeleine Albright, in a book entitled *Fascism: A Warning*, has declared that Donald Trump is the first "anti-democratic" president.[15] Yale philosophy professor Jason Stanley in *How Fascism Works: The Politics of Us and Them*, lumps Trump in with Hitler, genocidal mass murders in Rwanda, the Confederates, and the government of Myanmar.[16] "A leading Holocaust historian just compared the US to Nazi Germany" shrieked a headline on the neoliberal website *Vox* in October 2018.[17] The article referred to an essay in the *New York Review of Books* by the historian Christopher Browning. In addition to making the usual comparison of Trump to Hitler, Browning displayed his supercilious erudition by comparing Republican Senate majority leader Mitch McConnell to Hitler's predecessor and enabler German president Paul von Hindenburg.[18]

But even Browning's clever comparison of McConnell to von Hindenburg draws from the stock of trite Nazi equivalence arguments. Surely other enterprising academics could draw parallels between contemporary politicians they despise and fascists less well-known than Hitler and Mussolini. Why not ransack interwar European history to declare that Boris Johnson is the new Miklós Horthy (Hungary) or that Matteo Salvini is the new Antonio de Oliveira Salazar (Portugal)? Granted, asserting that Donald Trump is the new Engelbert Dollfuss (Austria) does not make him seem very frightening.

The most frequently cited evidence that Trump is a crypto-Nazi would-be dictator relied on his statements following violence in Charlottesville, Virginia, on August 12, 2017. A riot was provoked by neo-Nazis and other far-right groups who had gathered to protest the removal of a statue of Confederate general Robert E. Lee, a decision that had been made in the aftermath of the earlier mass murders committed by a white supremacist, Dylann Roof, at an African American church in Charlottesville on June 17. During the turmoil, a white supremacist drove his car into a crowd, killing a young woman.

In his initial statement following the riot, made in an impromptu press conference while he was on vacation, Trump did what most chief executives would do, condemning bigotry and calling for an end to violence. Many of Trump's detractors made the far-fetched claim that by not explicitly condemning white supremacy in his initial remarks, he was secretly signaling his approval of white nationalism. The transcripts of his initial remarks, and those of subsequent official statements and press conferences, in which he condemned white nationalism explicitly, provide no evidence for this conspiracy theory. August 12: "But we're closely following the terrible events unfolding in Charlottesville, Virginia. We condemn in the strongest possible terms this egregious display of hatred, bigotry and violence on many sides, on many sides. . . . Above all else, we must remember this truth: No matter our color, creed, religion or political party, we are all Americans first."[19] August 14: "Racism is evil. And those who cause violence in its name are criminals and thugs, including the KKK, neo-Nazis, white supremacists, and other hate groups that are repugnant to everything we hold dear as Americans."[20] August 15: "I'm not talking about the neo-Nazis and white nationalists because they should be condemned totally."[21]

Trump's critics tendentiously claimed that in denouncing violence on all sides he was asserting a moral equivalence between racism and antiracism. According to the *Washington Post*, among other news outlets, there was indeed "violence on many sides," as far-left counterprotesters belonging to groups like Antifa engaged in "swinging sticks, punching and spraying chemicals. Others threw balloons filled with paint or ink at the white nationalists. Everywhere, it seemed violence was exploding. The police did not move to break up the fights."[22]

Was Trump correct that many Americans who were not white supremacists opposed the removal of Confederate statues in Charlottesville and elsewhere? Polls following the incident showed that a majority of Americans disapproved of removing Confederate statues.[23] According to an NPR/PBS NewsHour/Marist poll of August 17, 2017, when given the choice between allowing Confederate statues to "remain as a historical symbol" or "be removed because they are offensive to some people," the only two political factions in the American population in which majorities said that the statutes should be removed were those who identified themselves as "very liberal–Liberal" (57 percent) or "strong Democrats" (57 percent). Strikingly, even 34 percent of these "strong Democrats" and 31 percent of "very liberal–Liberal" respondents opposed removal. A majority of "soft Democrats" favored leaving the statues in place (52–33, with 15 percent undecided). Among African American respondents, more favored leaving Confederate statues in place as historical symbols (44 percent) than removing them as offensive (40 percent); 16 percent were unsure.[24]

Trump had a history of making bigoted and inflammatory remarks. But no impartial historian who read the transcripts of Trump's statements would conclude that the president of the United States was secretly sending coded messages of approval for the very white supremacists whom he overtly and explicitly denounced. Phrases from his remarks were taken out of context, recombined and misconstrued so they could fit into the Trump-is-Hitler narrative peddled by many Democrats and anti-Trump Republicans—a narrative as deranged as the conspiracy theory that Trump was installed in the White House by Putin to serve as a Russian agent of influence.

THE VILLAINS OF the transatlantic establishment's antipopulist narrative are new, but the rhetoric of elite antipopulism itself is more than half a century old. Those who explain populism in politics as nothing more than the manipulation of individual bigotry or status anxiety by Hitlerian demagogues are recycling journalistic clichés and dubious scholarship from the mid-twentieth century.

The origins of today's antipopulist propaganda can be traced to *The Authoritarian Personality*, a book published in 1950 by a team of scholars including Theodor W. Adorno. Adorno was a member of the Frankfurt School, a group of émigré intellectuals from Nazi Germany. Having lived through the rise of National Socialism, these thinkers, many of them Jewish as well as Marxist, sought to understand how some members of the German proletariat, instead of behaving as Marxist theory predicted, had been susceptible to Hitler's anti-Semitism.

Even as an explanation of the Nazi phenomenon, this approach was misguided. Overall the German working class was one of the groups that supported the Nazis the least. Hitler's biographer Volker Ullrich observes: "The NSDAP was thus essentially a middle-class movement, and the proportion of university graduates, students and professors in

Munich was striking. Conversely, despite the fact that their propaganda was explicitly directed at blue-collar workers, the Nazis did not do well with that demographic group."[25] The urban working class, which favored social democrats and communists, like Catholic Germans, was consistently underrepresented among Hitler's supporters, who were disproportionately university graduates, civil servants, small business owners, inhabitants of small towns, and Protestants. Unpopular with the German working class, Hitler quickly crushed labor unions and rounded up their leaders upon seizing power.

Influenced by then-fashionable Freudian psychology, which few psychologists in our own time take seriously, Adorno and his colleagues tried to explain the appeal of fascism in terms of individual psychopathology. To test the susceptibility of individuals to fascist demagogy, Adorno and colleagues devised a personality test in 1947, including a measure called the California F Scale ("F" standing for Fascism). The test was supposed to measure latent fascist propensities along multiple vague dimensions, many of which were connected with fascism only in the minds of mid-twentieth century Marxists, like "Conventionalism. Rigid adherence to conventional, middle-class values" and "Sex. Exaggerated concern with sexual 'goings on.'"[26]

The test has generated a number of imitations, each as amateurish and pseudoscientific as the original. In 1996, the Canadian psychologist Bob Altemeyer warned that the US and Canada were ripe for fascism: "If my findings have shown me anything, they have revealed that what happened in Germany in 1933 can happen in North America too. Many people are already disposed to support a fascist overthrow of democracy."[27] Altemeyer's right-wing authoritarianism (RWA) test devised in 1981 purports to identify authoritarian tendencies on the basis of responses to questions that include these: "The 'old-fashioned ways' and the 'old-fashioned values' still show the best way to live" and "There is absolutely nothing wrong with nudist camps."[28] Those who prefer old-fashioned values to fads and nudist camps are defined as "authoritarians."

The C-Scale test, purporting to measure conservatism, created by Glenn Wilson and John Patterson in the 1960s, used attitudes toward jazz as a touchstone.[29] Combining the work of Altemeyer, Wilson, and Patterson, we may conclude that individuals who dislike both jazz and nudist camps are authoritarian conservatives. (Ironically, Adorno himself wrote a number of essays expressing his deep loathing of jazz music, declaring that "jazz can be easily adapted for use by fascism.")[30] Equally tendentious is the "rigidity of the right" model, which purports to prove that, in the words of one critic, liberals are "open and tolerant," while conservatives are "close-minded and intolerant and scared of everything."[31]

T HE AUTHORITARIAN PERSONALITY theory was first weaponized in American partisan politics in the 1950s. In *The New American Right* (1955), Daniel Bell, Nathan Glazer, Peter Viereck, and others explained McCarthyism as an anti-intellectual revolt of working-class Americans afflicted by status anxiety.[32] One of the contributors to *The New American Right* was the historian Richard Hofstadter, who adopted the term "pseudo-conservative" from the Adorno school.[33]

In several influential books and essays, Hofstadter tried

to rewrite the history of the New Deal by downplaying the importance of organized farmers and organized industrial workers in order to make college-educated professional reformers the heroes of twentieth-century American history. To put it another way, Hofstadter sought to define the New Deal as a system based not on democratic pluralism under a broker state, but on top-down technocracy. Nils Gilman observes: "If populism as a general political phenomenon was a byword for the wrong sort of politics, anti-Communist liberals at the apogee of their mid-century technocratic self-confidence believed that 'the right kind of revolution' would be elite-led and technocratic—precisely what Hofstadter believed he saw foreshadowed in the Progressive movement, with its commitment to scientific management, evidence-based public policy, credentialing and professionalization, education as a mode of social control, and the idea of best practices (then called 'one best system')."[34]

As part of his project of rewriting America as a story of rational technocratic reform threatened by dangerous democracy, Hofstadter misled a generation of readers into thinking that the American agrarian populist crusade of the 1890s had been an essentially anti-Semitic and protofascist movement.[35] Jon Wiener writes that Hofstadter "saw Joe McCarthy as a potential American Hitler and believed he had found the roots of American fascism among rural Protestants in the Midwest. It was history by analogy—but the analogy didn't work."[36] The erroneous thesis that McCarthyism was the rebirth of agrarian populism was refuted by a number of historians, including C. Vann Woodward in his 1959 essay "The Populist Heritage and the Intellectual."[37] In

1967, the fatal blow to Hofstadter's application of Adorno's status anxiety theory was delivered by Michael Paul Rogin, who showed in *The Intellectuals and McCarthy: The Radical Specter* that McCarthy's major supporters were suburban upper-middle-class Republicans, not rural populists.[38]

Although he was a poor historian, Hofstadter was awarded two Pulitzer Prizes for telling complacent, affluent elites in metropolitan enclaves what they wanted to hear about the alleged menace posed by the less-educated rabble. In a 1966 essay, Hofstadter coined a phrase, "the paranoid style in American politics," which to this day is invoked by lazy journalists and thinly educated pundits, most of them neoliberals or establishment conservatives, to delegitimate leftists as well as populists or conservatives with working-class or rural constituents.[39]

In the 1960s, the rhetoric of "pseudo-conservatism" and "status anxiety" and "the authoritarian personality" was revived again by centrist Democrats and some moderate Republicans to smear the followers of the conservative Republican presidential candidate Barry Goldwater in 1964 as potential fascists. So many academic American psychologists and psychiatrists declared the Republican candidate for president mentally unstable that the American Psychological Association in 1973 was compelled to enact a "Goldwater Rule" forbidding members from diagnosing politicians they did not like from a distance.

Like Trump in 2016, Goldwater in 1964 was viewed by many not only as mentally unbalanced but also as a dangerous potential tyrant who threatened American democracy. Ironically, Goldwater—a libertarian who had voted against the Civil Rights Act of 1964, though he had voted for previous civil rights laws—ended his long career as a pariah in the Republican Party, denounced by many conservatives because of his support for gay rights and environmentalism and his denunciation of the religious right. Recent historians have shown that Goldwater Republicanism owed more to the interests and values of the rising Sun Belt professional class and business elite than to working-class populists.[40]

IN 2001 IN *The International Journal of Political Psychology*, John Levi Martin concluded that "*The Authoritarian Personality* is probably the most deeply flawed work of prominence in political psychology" and should be regarded "as a cautionary example of bias."[41]

Unfortunately, instead of being ridiculed and forgotten, this long-discredited pseudoscience is endlessly recycled and dumped into the stream of public discourse. In an essay entitled "Trump's Fascist Efforts to Demolish Democracy," Professor Henry Giroux of the Department of English and Cultural Studies of McMaster University stitched together all of the clichés: "Trump has unleashed what Frankfurt School theorist Theodor Adorno once called an 'authoritarian personality,' the dark and menacing underside of a racist and totalitarian psychology and politics. Trump may not be Adolf Hitler, but there are disturbing similarities in his language and reactionary policies."[42] In January 2016, *Politico* published an essay by a PhD candidate in political science, Matthew MacWilliams, entitled "The One Weird Trait That Predicts Whether You're a Trump Supporter": "That's right, Trump's electoral strength—and his staying power—have been buoyed, above all, by Americans with authoritarian in-clinations."[43]

According to Pippa Norris, a Harvard political scientist: "Authoritarian values are those which uphold belief in a strong leader, in a strong state, and in robust law and order. These are traditional values like the family, home, religion, and then a variety of other values like nativism, the importance of national unity, the national community versus outsiders whether defined by nationality or ethnicity or race."[44]

It is worth pausing to reflect on how bizarre it is to call attitudes shared by most people in every society "authoritar-ian." Even in the most liberal and democratic of liberal de-mocracies, most citizens prefer strong leaders to weak leaders, a strong state to a feeble government, and "robust law and order" to—what? Weak and ineffective law and order? Ram-pant crime?

Norris's list of "authoritarian values" continues. It in-cludes "the family, home, religion" and "the importance of national unity" and "national community, whether defined by nationality or ethnicity or race." For Norris and like-minded scholars, ordinary patriots who are committed to their nation-states, even if their national patriotism is anti-racist and liberal and democratic, are "authoritarians" along with far-right white supremacists who dream of racially pure "ethnostates" created by ethnic cleansing or genocide. Nor-ris's nonauthoritarian citizen, who is unpatriotic and indif-ferent to national unity, tolerant of lawlessness and disorder, and puts little value on family, would strike most people as an amoral sociopath.

Noting the immortality of "Richard Hofstadter's famous

catchphrase, the 'paranoid style in American politics,'" the historian Leo P. Ribuffo wrote in 2017: "As someone who has tried to hammer in the stake for several decades, I can't help noticing that the term has again risen from the grave as in a horror movie populated not by vampires, zombies and terrified teenagers, but by Donald Trump, superficial pundits, and terrified liberals and radicals."[45] As it has done since World War II, the overclass intelligentsia in the future is likely to continue to portray critics of technocratic neoliberalism as irrational and maladjusted, for the reason explained by the historian Norman Pollack in a critique of Richard Hofstadter's work in 1960:

> Basically, psychology imposes a static model of society (in effect, the consensus framework) upon the study of social movements because it requires a standard or reference point by which to judge what is or is not irrational. Thus, all behavior not conforming to the model is categorized as irrational, with the result that the analysis is biased in favor of the status quo and places all protest movements by definition at a disadvantage.[46]

The appropriation of terms from psychology to discredit political opponents is part of the modern therapeutic culture that the sociologist Christopher Lasch criticized.[47] Along with the concept of the authoritarian personality, the term "-phobe" for political opponents has been added to the arsenal of obloquy deployed by technocratic neoliberals against those who disagree with them. The coinage of the term "homophobia" by the psychologist George Weinberg in the 1970s has been followed by a proliferation of pseudoclinical terms in which those who hold viewpoints at variance with the left-libertarian social consensus of the transatlantic ruling class are understood to suffer from "phobias" of various kinds similar to the psychological disorders of agoraphobia (fear of open spaces), ornithophobia (fear of birds), and pentheraphobia (fear of one's mother-in-law). The most famous use of this rhetorical strategy can be found in then-candidate Hillary Clinton's leaked confidential remarks to an audience of donors at a fund-raiser in New York in 2016: "You know, to just be grossly generalistic, you could put half of Trump's supporters into what I call the basket of deplorables. Right? They're racist, sexist, homophobic, xenophobic, Islamophobic—you name it."[48]

A disturbed young man who is driven by internal compulsions to harass and assault gay men is obviously different from a learned Orthodox Jewish rabbi who is kind to lesbians and gay men as individuals but opposes homosexuality, along with adultery, premarital sex, and masturbation, on theological grounds—but both are "homophobes." A racist who opposes large-scale immigration because of its threat to the supposed ethnic purity of the national majority is obviously different from a non-racist trade unionist who thinks that immigrant numbers should be reduced to create tighter labor markets to the benefit of workers—but both are "xenophobes." A Christian fundamentalist who believes that Muslims are infidels who will go to hell is obviously different from an atheist who believes that all religion is false—but both are "Islamophobes." This blurring of important distinctions is not an accident. The purpose of describing political adversaries as "-phobes" is to medicalize politics and treat differing viewpoints as evidence of mental and emotional disorders.

In the latter years of the Soviet Union, political dissidents were often diagnosed with "sluggish schizophrenia" and then confined to psychiatric hospitals and drugged. According to the regime, anyone who criticized communism literally had to be insane.[49] If those in today's West who oppose the dominant consensus of technocratic neoliberalism are in fact emotionally and mentally disturbed, to the point that their maladjustment makes it unsafe to allow them to vote, then to be consistent, neoliberals should support the involuntary confinement, hospitalization, and medication of Trump voters and Brexit voters and other populist voters for their own good, as well as the good of society.

IN REALITY, POLITICS does not imitate sensational thriller fiction. US president Donald Trump and British prime minister Boris Johnson and Britain's Labour Party leader Jeremy Corbyn are not Russian agents of influence installed by Moscow in pursuit of a sinister grand design to overthrow liberal democracy in the West and the world. Even so, the Russian government, like all major countries, employs intelligence operatives whose actions should be monitored and thwarted when they go beyond the low-level activities tolerated by both sides in modern great power relations.

The United States and the established democracies of Western Europe in the twenty-first century do not resemble in any significant way the unstable Weimar Republic that was overthrown by Hitler and replaced by a militaristic, genocidal, totalitarian state. Even so, there are genuine neo-Nazis and other white supremacists in the West, including the American mass murderers Timothy McVeigh, Dylann Roof, and Patrick Crusius. Police and intelligence agencies in the US and Europe should do their best to identify genuine potential domestic and foreign terrorists and prevent them from doing harm.

Liberal democracy in the West today is not endangered by Russian machinations or resurgent fascism. But liberalism and democracy alike are endangered when irrational moral panics like today's Russia Scare and Brown Scare in the West lead hysterical elites to redefine "extremism" or "fascism" or "white nationalism" to include ordinary populists, conservatives, libertarians, and heterodox leftists. What the historian Louis Hartz in *The Liberal Tradition in America* wrote of McCarthyite conservatives in the 1950s who feared that many of their fellow citizens were Russian dupes or dangerous communists who needed to be censored and blacklisted applies with equal force to today's paranoid establishmentarians who fear that many of their fellow citizens are Russian dupes or dangerous fascists: "What must be accounted one of the tamest, mildest and most unimaginative majorities in modern political history has been bound down by a set of restrictions that betray fanatical terror."[50]

My purpose is not to defend populist demagogy, which can be harmful and destructive without being totalitarian or traitorous. Contemporary populism is a kind of convulsive autoimmune response by the body politic to the chronic degenerative disease of oligarchy. The greatest threat to liberal democracy on both sides of the Atlantic is not its imminent overthrow by meme-manipulating masterminds in Moscow or by white nationalists who seek to create a Fourth Reich. The greatest threat to Western democracy is the gradual decay of North America and Europe under well-educated, well-mannered, and well-funded centrist neoliberal politicians into something like the regimes that have long been familiar in many Latin American countries and the American South, in which oppressive oligarchic rule provokes destructive populist revolts.

Weimar Republic? No. Banana republic? Maybe.

CHAPTER SEVEN

The Workerless Paradise: The Inadequacy of Neoliberal Reform

NOT ALL MEMBERS OF embattled Western over-classes have interpreted populist political insur-rections against the establishment parties as proof of Russian conspiracies or the revival of fascism. Some members of the transatlantic elite recognize that some, if not all, populist voter grievances are legitimate. The alternative to simply dismissing populist voters as gullible dupes hypnotized by homegrown Hitlers or Muscovite masterminds is co-optation—attempts to rescue as much of the technocratic neoliberal order as possible, by making selective reforms of trade, immigration, tax, or wage policies to win the support of alienated voters and deprive populist demagogues of their constituents.

In some cases this might work. Danish Social Democrats, for example, have reversed their political decline by adopting a more restrictive immigration policy, winning back voters motivated by that issue who had cast protest votes for populist parties.[1] In other cases, ameliorative new social insurance programs might reduce some of the insecurity many workers feel in the unfriendly new economy created by neoliberalism.

But the willingness of Western elites to refrain from imposing their deeply held left-libertarian values on their fellow citizens or to pay higher taxes to bribe the masses below them is undoubtedly limited. And if redistribution of income or assets were not accompanied by redistribution of power, the feelings of powerlessness that drive much working-class anger would remain.

THE IMPLICIT THEORY of technocratic neoliberalism is that the US and other Western societies at this point are essentially classless societies in which the only significant barriers involve race and gender. The people at the top got there purely as a result of their own efforts, on the basis of their superior intellectual or academic skills. Many of these corporate managers, financiers, lawyers, accountants, engineers, foundation program officers, media elites, and academics do pretty much the same kind of work that people in their professions did half a century ago, adjusted for differences in technology and industrial organization. But we are supposed to believe that they are not just old-fashioned managers and professionals, but members of a new "creative class" and "digital elite," the "thinkpreneurs" and "thought leaders" of the "knowledge economy" who live in "brain hubs" (to use only a few of the flattering terms in the lexicon of overclass self-idolatry).

From the assumption that a nearly meritocratic "knowledge economy" has replaced class-stratified, bureaucratic managerial capitalism follow two kinds of policies. The first are class-neutral, race- or gender-based policies to remove barriers to the advancement of racial minorities and women, including native white women. The second are policies that include skills training or retraining for unsuccessful native white men.

Class-neutral, race-based policies in the United States include affirmative action in hiring, government set-asides for specified groups in contracting, and gerrymandering of congressional districts to create majority-minority districts likely to elect a member of a racial minority as a representative. In most cases the beneficiaries of these policies tend to be members of the affluent elite within a particular racial or ethnic group. For technocratic neoliberalism, the goal is to ensure that there is the proper racial and gender balance within the overclass, the balance that presumably would result from a perfect meritocracy. If pure meritocracy does not yet exist, then a simulacrum will be created. But as the British socialist thinker Ralph Miliband put it, "access to positions of power by members of the subordinate classes does not change the fact of domination; it only changes the personnel."[2]

The assumption that contemporary North America and Europe already have near-classless societies, to be made perfectly classless by a few low-cost policy interventions, also compels neoliberals to attribute the problems of the native white Western working class not to the class system but rather to personal shortcomings, which a number of unfortunate individuals are alleged to share.

The most important personal shortcoming is alleged to be a lack of adequate job skills. The theory of skill-biased technological change (SBTC) was popular during the bubble years before the Great Recession. SBTC theory explained rising inequality by asserting that the "left-behind" members of the working class had inferior and outmoded skills not needed by the "creative class" or the "digital elite" in the new "global knowledge economy."

The premise has been that US corporations like Apple did not offshore production to China to take advantage of low-wage, unfree workers and state subsidies of various kinds. No, it is often implied, the poor Chinese workers migrating from rural areas to make iPhones in sweatshop factories in southern China in degrading conditions for a pittance had superior STEM (Science, Technology, Engineering, and Math) skills unmatched among ignorant American or European workers. Provide these "left-behind" workers in the West with appropriate skills ("human capital" in the pseudoeconomic jargon of neoliberalism) and their earnings will increase.

O N THE BASIS of SBTC theory, school curricula in the US and elsewhere have been reconfigured to focus on STEM skills. For a generation, the conventional wisdom has held that the "jobs of the future" are "knowledge economy" jobs like software coding. But is this really true?

The Bureau of Labor Statistics (BLS) of the US Department of Commerce has provided estimates for US job growth between 2016 and 2026. When the fastest-growing occupations are examined, the knowledge economy thesis does indeed appear to be partly true: "statisticians," "software developers, applications," and "mathematicians" are seventh, ninth, and tenth in the list, respectively, although these are outranked by solar photovoltaic installers, wind turbine service technicians (construction and maintenance jobs), and home health and personal care aides.

However, many of these fast-growing jobs are growing rapidly from tiny bases (the list also includes "bicycle repairers"). What about occupations with the greatest absolute number of job openings? Here the only STEM job category among the top ten is "software developers, applications" at number four, paying $101,790 a year. The other categories with the most openings in the US are personal care aides; combined food preparation and serving workers, including fast food; registered nurses; home health aides; janitors and cleaners, except maids and housekeeping cleaners; general and operations managers; laborers and freight, stock, and material movers; medical assistants; and waiters and waitresses.

Among these non-STEM jobs, only two pay relatively well—general and operations managers ($100,410) and registered nurses ($70,000). These happen to be the only two that require college degrees, according to the BLS. None of the other jobs with the greatest absolute growth in the US pay more than the annual salary of a medical assistant ($32,480).[3]

If the "new economy" or "knowledge economy" primarily rewarded education, rather than ownership of assets, then we would expect the greatest increase in incomes to have occurred among the top 30 percent with at least a bachelor's degree. Instead, the gains from growth have been concentrated among those with income from capital—investors and managers with stock options.[4]

In one study, in sixteen Western democracies labor productivity grew far more rapidly than average real wages and fringe benefits, but most income growth went to profits of owners and shareholders.[5] Another study of thirteen advanced capitalist countries found that the growth in real wages, which had been 4 percent in the 1970s, was less than 1 percent between 1980 and 2005, while the wage share of income declined from 78 percent to 63 percent, with the rest going to income from profits, interest, dividends, and rents.[6] The big money is not in "human capital" but in plain old-fashioned capital. The new economy is really a new version of the old economy—the managerial capitalist economy, not some mythical, immaterial "knowledge economy."

To be sure, nations with large pools of engineers and scientists are likely to do better than those without them. Even so, there are relatively few "knowledge economy" jobs as a share of the total. And the well-paid and prestigious ones that are not offshored in the future or given to foreign indentured servants like H-1B guest workers in the US who are willing to work for lower wages than natives will be highly prized, in competitions that the affluent offspring of over-class families are likely to win. The greatest payoffs as a rule will continue to go to investors, bankers, and CEOs, not engineers or scientists.

For working-class Americans and Europeans, the jobs of the future are mostly low-wage jobs, many of them in health care. In most of these jobs, the low wages are caused not by a lack of university education, which is not needed, nor by a lack of vocational skills, but by a lack of bargaining power on the part of workers.

A LONG WITH GREATER access to higher education, geographic relocation is another neoliberal panacea. In addition to telling working-class citizens they need to learn to code, the purveyors of the conventional wisdom sometimes tell them they need to move to the San Francisco Bay Area or other high-tech hubs where many software coders are found.

Influenced by "Why Do Cities Matter?"—a 2015 study by the economists Chang-Tai Hsieh and Enrico Moretti—many business journalists and pundits have argued that the US could be more productive if land-use restrictions allowed more workers to move to cities such as San Francisco, San Jose, New York, Boston, and Seattle. The grain of truth in this notion is that agglomeration effects help certain cities dominate particular industries and professions.

Lost in the hype, however, has been the important qualification of Hsieh and Moretti: "The assumption of inter-industry mobility is clearly false in the short run."[7] In other words, neither personal nor national productivity will necessarily be raised if a roboticist moves to Wall Street or a stockbroker moves to Silicon Valley. Meanwhile, a janitor or home health aide who moves from a small town to either New York City or the Bay Area to practice the same trade could be worse off because of the higher cost of living.

S O MUCH FOR the neoliberal establishment panaceas of higher education, retraining, and geographic mobility. Somewhat bolder proposals to help the working class, which also avoid any heretical questioning of the labor market effects of deunionization, offshoring, and mass immigration, include more redistribution of income in the form of cash transfers or tax breaks and more opportunities for working-class citizens to start their own businesses.

Redistributionist proposals range from expanding tax subsidies to wage earners, like America's earned income tax credit (EITC), to the old but periodically revived idea of a universal basic income (UBI), which would allow all citizens to live at a minimally adequate level without working. While some minor forms of enhanced redistribution to mollify discontented voters will undoubtedly be tried in many Western countries, proposals for massive cash transfers are doomed for a number of reasons.

Purchasing political acquiescence from workers who have stagnant or declining incomes with substantial amounts of cash requires an economically dynamic sector of the economy to make the bribes affordable. In some versions, radical redistributionism posits the permanent existence of high intellectual-property rents flowing from the rest of the world to tech tycoons, along with global financial rents flowing to money managers. These rents, it is assumed, will be so high and sustainable that the tycoons and money managers will gladly share them with the rest of the population in the nation-states in which they happen to reside.

At the local level, something like this system has long existed in tech centers like San Francisco and financial entrepôts like New York and London. Local rentier interests are coddled by governments in return for their contribution to revenues. But while it may work in a few hub cities, the policy cannot be scaled up to the level of the ordinary nation-state, much less a continental nation-state like the United States, with a third of a billion inhabitants.

It is no coincidence that Reaganism-Clintonism and Thatcherism-Blairism flourished in an era of prolonged asset bubbles. For a time, it is possible for stock market booms and real estate bubbles to fund public services and redistribution while allowing the wealthy to keep most of their gains. But the financial industry is volatile and global innovation rents quickly disappear, as a result of lapsing patents, intellectual property theft, foreign success in indigenous innovation, and the commoditization of former cutting-edge industries.

Furthermore, there are too many opportunities for evasive tax arbitrage. Which billionaires and firms will consent to be taxed to pay for these massive schemes of national redistribution? The ones who hide their wealth in the Cayman Islands, or others, perhaps, who hide it in Panama or Jersey or Switzerland?

Can other sources of revenue pay for massive, permanent cash transfers to the working class as well as the poor? A "robot tax" has been endorsed by French socialist Benoît Hamon and American capitalist Bill Gates, to fund a UBI as a solution to the as-yet-nonexistent problem of mass technological unemployment. But if robots were cheap and common enough to cause mass unemployment, the commoditized robot industry might not generate enough profit to support a massively expanded welfare state; you might as well try to pay for a universal basic income with a microwave oven tax. If, on the other hand, robots were scarce and selling for a premium, technological unemployment would not be a problem—and the robot tax perversely would encourage the substitution of low-wage workers for advanced machines, putting the Industrial Revolution into reverse.

Nor can a few niche advanced manufacturing sectors pay for the massive redistribution from the few to the many required by the redistribution strategy. The incentive to invest to increase productivity in manufacturing and services at home is undermined by neoliberal trade policies that boost profits more easily through the offshoring of high-value-added production and low-value-added activities alike. Even worse, in the nontraded domestic service sector, flooding the low-end labor market with poorly paid and poorly educated immigrants reduces the incentive of service industries to increase their productivity by investing in labor-saving technology or reorganizing their business models to minimize the employment of unskilled labor.

In short, neoliberal economic strategy itself, because of its bias in favor of business models relying on cheap labor at home and abroad, tends to undermine the domestic productivity growth needed to pay for the massive redistribution that, it is hoped, would align the interests of workers and managerial elites.

It is no surprise that greatly expanded redistribution is supported by many Silicon Valley investors and executives who hope that more transfer payments may anesthetize the population to the pain of low wages and rising inequality.[8] Marx called religion "the opiate of the masses." In redistribution, the managerial elite has found a new opiate.

Or maybe not. In the unlikely event that a UBI was adopted by any country, it might create enormous political pressure on the part of many voters to drastically cut even reasonable levels of legal immigration in order to prevent the country from becoming a welfare magnet. In addition, families with one or a few children might denounce families with many children for diluting shares of the national dole. Advocates for the poor might try to increase UBI amounts by means-testing the giveaway, turning the affluent into enemies of the program. Far from ending class war and promoting social justice, in politics a UBI might well incite a Hobbesian war of all against all.

RECENTLY A RIVAL approach to reform, antimonopolism, has attracted growing attention and support among American progressives.[9] Based on a revival of the long-moribund small-producer republicanism of William Jennings Bryan, Louis Brandeis, and Wright Patman, this school blames inequality and a host of other social ills on increasing "concentration" or "monopoly" and proposes a radical antitrust policy as a panacea. Breaking up large firms into smaller ones, it is claimed, will increase opportunities for Americans to exit the labor market by transitioning from wage earners to small business owners. Those who continue to sell their labor for wages will have their bargaining power increased, and the monopsony wage-setting power of employers reduced, by a government policy of breaking up big employers into a greater number of smaller ones—so it is said.

Praising small business is certain to be an applause line in most Western democracies, given popular nostalgia for old-fashioned small-town and rural life. But multiplying the number of small firms will not help the wage-earning majority, because small firms pay poorly. In the US, large firms with over five hundred workers in 2007 employed 44 percent of all workers but only 28 percent of low-wage workers. Firms with fewer than ten workers employed only 20 percent of the workforce but 42 percent of low-wage workers.[10]

Some of the new antimonopolists have suggested that breaking up big firms can increase the bargaining power of workers. But the idea that janitors will be in a better position to bargain for higher wages if Facebook is broken into three or four or five giant successor firms is implausible, to say the least.

In the US, firms with more than five hundred employees account for 51.5 percent of all employment.[11] To increase worker bargaining power, should each firm with five hundred employees be broken up into two firms of 250 employees, or ten firms of fifty workers? What about one hundred firms of five workers apiece? Compared to more direct pro-labor measures like minimum wages, collective bargaining and limits on global labor arbitrage, pulverizing the most productive firms in the economy is a very roundabout and inefficient way to try to raise wages, like burning down a barn to roast a pig in the famous fable by Charles Lamb.[12]

Like redistributionism, antimonopolism cannot work at the national level in today's system of liberalized trade and globalized production. If the Justice Department used antitrust to break up large suppliers in the US, firms that coordinate global supply chains could simply shift those links in production to foreign countries with more lenient competition policies. The result could be accelerated by American deindustrialization, with further massive shifts in employment from the traded sector to the low-wage, low-productivity domestic service sector. In some cases, foreign state-backed national champions might win US domestic market share from American firms that had been broken up by the federal government. Just as a UBI cannot work without stringent and strictly enforced limits on immigration, so a neo-Brandeisian antimonopoly policy cannot work except in a much more protectionist and autarkic US economy, which could only be created by measures that cosmopolitan, open-borders progressives, like their newfound libertarian allies in matters of trade and immigration, would be sure to denounce as xenophobic, racist, and nativist.

THE CURE-ALLS OF education, redistribution, and antimonopolism enjoy broad elite support from the center-left to the center-right, in part, no doubt, because they do not question the commitment of post-1970s neoliberalism to liberalized policies about trade, immigration, and organized labor. Redistribution, for example, is not necessarily a left-wing idea. On the contrary, labor liberals and social democrats have usually opposed proposals for posttax transfers of cash to individuals, in favor of measures that increase the ability of workers to bargain for higher pretax wages, like limits on immigration and offshoring, collective bargaining at the firm or sectoral level, and public job guarantees and socialized in-kind benefits like universal health care ("decommodification").

Conversely, cash transfers and ideas of universal capitalism have a long and distinguished pedigree on the free market right. From Milton Friedman in the 1960s to Charles Murray in the 1990s, libertarians have proposed using some form of a basic income as a substitute, not a supplement, for most or all other social insurance and antipoverty programs.[13]

Like the panaceas of education and redistribution, antimonopolism does not question the premises of economic neoliberalism. Indeed, the antimonopolists claim, with some justification, that they are even more fervent devotees of markets than conventional neoliberals. "Make Markets Be Markets" was the title of a campaign by the center-left Roosevelt Institute. The leading new antimonopolist think tank is named the Open Markets Institute. Like homeopathic medicine, all of these alleged cures treat the ills of the market with doses of more market.

Worst of all, three of these schools of thought seek to respond to working-class populist rebellions by offering workers the chance to become something other than workers, as though there were something shameful and retrograde about being an ordinary wage earner. Many champions of education as a panacea want to turn wage earners into professionals. Advocates of universal capitalism want to turn wage earners into investors. Antimonopolists want to turn wage earners into small business owners.

In the 1930s, Keynes speculated about the euthanasia of the rentier class. These reformers propose the euthanasia of the working class. The neoliberal utopia is a workerless paradise.

WHAT ABOUT SOCIALISM—the genuine kind with state ownership of the means of production? In theory, the option of democratic socialism need not be discredited by the horrors wrought by Marxist-Leninist dictatorships in rural nations like twentieth-century Russia and China.

Democratic socialism is discredited for other reasons. One is the greater track record of the mixed economy, with a blend of markets, public enterprises, and nonprofit provision, over both the pure free market economy and state socialism. A case can be made for socializing some enterprises or industries, but socializing everything can only be justified by dogmatic ideology.

The other argument against democratic socialism is the fact that socializing most or all of the economy by itself would not address the problem of checking the power of the managerial elite, which mere elections, however free, would be unlikely to constrain. Empowering organized labor by means like tripartite business-labor-government bargaining can provide real checks on the managerial overclass, without sacrificing the dynamism of the mixed economy.

THE AMERICAN WRITER Daniel McCarthy has aptly called approaches like the ones I have criticized in this chapter "palliative liberalism."[14] However popular these miracle cures may be among the managerial elite and the overclass intelligentsia, as remedies for working-class distress in the deindustrialized heartlands of the Western world the panaceas of redistributionism, education, and antimonopolism are like prescriptions of aspirin for cancer. They may ameliorate the symptoms, but they do not cure the disease—the imbalance of power, within Western nation-states, between the overclass and the working class as a whole, including many exploited immigrant workers who labor for the affluent in the metropolitan hubs.

If banana republicanism is to be avoided as the fate of the Western democracies, reformers in America and Europe will have to do far more than buy off the population with a subsidy here or an antitrust lawsuit there. Indeed, if a package of minor, ameliorative reforms is handed down from the mountaintops of Davos or Aspen by a claque of benevolent billionaires and the technocrats and the politicians and intellectuals whom the billionaires subsidize, with little or no public participation or debate, the lack of voice and agency of most citizens will be made apparent in the most humiliating way.

What the racially and religiously diverse working-class majorities in the Western nations need is what they once possessed and no longer have: countervailing power. In the absence of mass-membership institutions comparable to the older grassroots parties, labor unions, and religious organizations, which can provide ordinary citizens with the collective power to check the abuses of the managerial elite, palliative reform at most can create oligarchy with a human face.

CHAPTER EIGHT

Countervailing Power: Toward a New Democratic Pluralism

ALMOST ALL OF THE political turmoil in Western Europe and North America can be explained by the new class war. The first class war in the West ended with the establishment of democratic pluralist systems on both sides of the Atlantic after World War II. Trade unions, participatory political parties, and religious and civic organizations compelled university-educated managerial elites to share power with them or defer to their values. Then, between the 1970s and the present, the terms of the uneasy democratic pluralist peace treaties between national working classes and national managerial elites were unilaterally abrogated by the latter. No longer restrained by working-class power, the metropolitan overclass within Western democracies has run amok, provoking a belated populist rebellion from below that has been exploited, often with disastrous results, by demagogues, many of them opportunists from elite backgrounds, like Donald Trump and Boris Johnson.

Antisystem populism, the force behind the election of Donald Trump, the Brexit vote in Britain, and the rise of populist parties in continental Europe, has been triggered in different nations by different causes—deindustrialization here, immigration or tax policies there. But whatever the immediate stimulus, the underlying cause is the same—long-smoldering rage by non-college-educated workers against damage done to their economic bargaining power, political influence, and cultural dignity during the half-century revolution from above of technocratic neoliberalism.

The establishment response to populism threatens democracy more than populism itself. In responding to populist insurgencies, embattled Western establishments can follow two strategies: co-optation and repression. As we saw in the last chapter, most of the ideas that have been proposed for co-opting alienated populist voters and reconciling them to a more or less unchanged neoliberal economic order— massive after-tax redistribution schemes, using antitrust to multiply the number of small business owners, giving more citizens college diplomas for jobs that do not require them— are impractical, excessively expensive, or both.

Repression is cheaper than co-optation. It is easier for the managerial overclasses of the West simply to marginalize populist politicians who represent legitimate popular grievances in the name of combating one or another illusory menace to democracy: the supposed danger of a neo-Nazi takeover, or an alleged Russian plot to conquer the West by means of well-placed secret agents and the use of the Internet to hypnotize Western voters.

The danger facing modern societies is not that demagogues will trigger the mythical authoritarian personalities diagnosed by Adorno but rather that demagogues will exploit the very real condition of anomie or alienation diagnosed by Durkheim. Overclass establishments will then exaggerate the danger of populism to dismantle democracy, triggering a vicious cycle of oligarchic repression and demagogic disruption.

The alternative to both technocratic neoliberalism and demagogic populism is democratic pluralism. The essential insight of democratic pluralism is that electoral democracy is a necessary but not sufficient condition for democracy. Because the wealthy and educated inevitably tend to dominate all parties, if only through their personnel, "territorial" representation must be supplemented (not replaced) by occupational or communal "social federalism" (to use the language of the English pluralists of a century ago). To this end, substantial areas of policy should be delegated to rule-making institutions, which must represent particular portions of the community, like organized labor and business in wage-setting sectoral bodies, or representatives of religious and secular creeds in bodies charged with oversight of education and the media. The territorial state, as the only entity with coercive authority, should exercise oversight of all institutions and intervene if necessary to protect individual rights or other state interests. But in the democratic pluralist vision of democracy, the government in many areas should reign, not rule.

Far from being utopian, democratic pluralism is free from many of the defects of the definition of democracy in terms of formal electoral politics and public administration. For one thing, it does not require legislators to be omnicompetent generalists. While retaining oversight, legislatures can cede large areas of policy making to those with higher stakes and expertise.

Democratic pluralism magnifies the power of ordinary citizens by providing more than one mode of representation. They can be represented, not merely by politicians from arbitrarily defined political districts who are infrequently elected, but also by labor or business representatives in tripartite economic bodies or by members of their religious or cultural subculture in cultural commissions that represent diverse stakeholders. These non-legislative bodies can be representative, even though it is inappropriate to organize them as replicas democratic legislatures based on one person, one vote.

While institutionalized pluralism benefits society as a whole, it is particularly important for members of the working-class majority. Because they lack money and status, working-class people have only one source of power: their numbers. They can affect politics only through disciplined mass organizations answerable to them, of which the most important in the past have been mass-membership parties, trade unions, and churches. Whatever form they take, mass-membership organizations must have their own leaders, independent of other centers of power, even if many of the leaders themselves are drawn from college-educated families. In the words of David Marquand:

> The alternative power centres on which [pluralists] rely to check the power of the intrusive state must have a capacity for self defence. This means that they cannot be anarchistic communes. They too must be led, and leadership is elitist by definition. For plural-

ists, the notion that we can live in a world without elites is as fatuous and as dangerous as the notion that we can live in a world without power. If power checks power, elites countervail elites.[1]

The trade unions, party machines, and religious congregations of the past had their share of corruption, and so would their modern equivalents. Like all political systems, a democratic pluralist regime is vulnerable to "rent-seeking" by self-interested economic interests. But corruption is more easily exposed and contained in a system with a multitude of petty power brokers than in a centralized regime with a relatively small elite whose members tend to dominate the economy, the government, and the media.

If it is successful, democratic pluralism, by incorporating all classes and major subcultures to some degree in policy making in the market, government, and cultural sectors, can reduce the sense of isolation and powerlessness that opportunistic demagogues can exploit. While thwarting the oligarchic tendencies of technocratic neoliberalism, the restoration of democratic pluralism in the West might also forestall disruptive rebellions like Trumpism, Brexit, and the yellow vest revolt in France. Interclass tensions can be dissipated in thousands of small-scale negotiations, instead of accumulating until there is one huge explosion.

ALTHOUGH THE OLD parties, unions, and churches cannot be restored in their historic forms, the restoration of working-class power on both sides of the Atlantic requires the establishment of membership institutions to serve as their functional equivalents. These functional equivalents might be called the "guild" in the realm of the economy, the "ward" in the realm of government, and the "congregation" in the realm of culture. In the economic realm, the guild would exercise countervailing power on behalf of working-class citizens against employers and investors. In the realm of government, the ward would exercise countervailing power on behalf of working-class citizens against organized money and organized expertise. And in the realm of culture, the congregation would exercise countervailing power on behalf of working-class citizens against overclass media elites and overclass academic elites.

In the economy, a new class peace treaty to end the new class war would involve the restoration of tripartite bargaining among labor and capital in some form. As we saw in chapter 3, tripartism rejects the absurd nineteenth-century classical liberal idea that individual workers can bargain over wages or working conditions in any meaningful way with giant national or global corporations, banks, or chains.

At the same time, tripartism rejects the socialist panacea of government control of production. The tripartite approach also rejects excessive government micromanagement of minimum wages and working conditions using one-size-fits-all rules. Some minimum standards are necessary, but many decisions should be left to collective bargaining among organized capital and organized labor, brokered by national governments.

Tripartite institutions that enable business-labor negotiations over wages, working conditions, and investment decisions have always come in different forms that are appropriate in different sectors. The kind of collective bargaining most familiar to Americans, and most despised by managers, not without justification, is "enterprise bargaining"—the unionization of particular companies or particular work sites, one by one, in an adversarial and disruptive process. In other countries, collective bargaining among labor representatives and business representatives takes place at the national or regional level and results in decisions that are binding on all firms and labor organizations within a sector. Another alternative is codetermination of the kind adopted in postwar West Germany, the requirement that corporate boards include worker representatives.

Traditional union structures and methods like strikes fit poorly with many of today's service occupations. In Britain and other countries, as well as some states of the US, "wage boards" have been used to set wages and working conditions in so-called sweated industries, which have many small employers and low-wage workers and are difficult to unionize. Recently a wage board raised the minimum wage for fast-food workers in the state of New York. For many of today's dispersed service workers, representation on local or national wage boards, with representatives chosen by workers through elections or company works councils or other means, may be a more effective basis for government-brokered business-labor negotiation than old-fashioned, site-based collective bargaining.[2]

WHILE THE GOAL of democratic pluralist reform in the economy should be to create new "guilds" with genuine bargaining power in new forms of business-labor-government tripartism, in the realm of government and politics the goal should be a partial restoration of localism at the smallest level. To describe units of microdemocracy I have chosen the term "ward." Thomas Jefferson's benighted racial views and agrarian economics do not discredit his enthusiasm for "ward republics," or units small enough to permit ordinary people to experience politics as participants and not mere observers. Even if they have college degrees, local public officials from working-class families or with working-class constituents are likely to have greater sympathies for ordinary Americans and local communities than higher-status members of the managerial elite, clustered in a small number of major urban hubs.

Many political philosophers and social scientists have argued that there are diseconomies of scale in the civic and political realm when political units grow too large. The American political scientist Robert Dahl argued that the ideal political unit has between fifty thousand and several hundred thousand inhabitants.[3] As it happens, fifty thousand is more or less the size of the wards in the city of Chicago. In comparison, city council members in New York City each represent more than 164,000 constituents while in Los Angeles they represent 250,000.[4] Chicago's ward system is often given credit for integrating European immigrants as well as domestic migrants, such as African Americans from the South, into the urban power structure. Chicago is a deeply troubled city in many ways, mainly because of the social effects of deindustrialization. But the ward system is not to blame and a more centralized, elitist system dominated by donors, real estate developers, and technocrats would be worse.

Basic civil rights should be identical everywhere within a nation, and in a federal system social insurance is most efficiently handled at the national level. But there remain many local institutions that can be provided as amenities for all local residents—public clinics, public libraries and museums, city and county parks, even public golf courses, basketball and tennis courts, and swimming pools. To ensure that what Ganesh Sitaraman and Anne Alstott call "public options" like these are adequately funded even in poor localities, they should be financed by national revenue-sharing schemes allocated on a per capita basis for public goods to be chosen by local citizens.[5]

The rootedness of most working-class Americans and Europeans in their hometowns and regions is often lamented by the intellectuals of the managerial overclass: Why don't the lazy losers in heartland communities show some initiative and move to the Bay Area to invent an app, or relocate to London to work in finance? But the geographic immobility of the working class is both a political challenge, in a world of mobile capital, and a political opportunity—an opportunity to build multigenerational communities instead of transient labor camps.

In his book *Human Scale Revisited*, Kirkpatrick Sale quotes the British historian H. D. F. Kitto's fable about an Athenian citizen from the time of Pericles who visits the Athenian Club in London:

> The Greek replies, "How many clubs are there in London?" The member, at a guess, says about five hundred. The Greek then says, "Now if all these combined, what a splendid premises they would build. They could have a clubhouse as big as Hyde Park."

"But," says the member, "that would no longer be a club." "Precisely," says the Greek, "and a polis as big as yours is no longer a polis."[6]

Rebuilding democracy at the local level is not enough. In a post-neoliberal democratic pluralist regime, provincial and national legislatures must regain some of the power that they have lost to executives and judges.

Strengthening legislatures in which working-class majorities have at least some influence against overclass-dominated executive and judicial branches does not necessarily require formal constitutional reform. After all, the neoliberal revolution from above in the last half century in the West was carried out by managerial elites in parliamentary and presidential regimes and countries with proportional representation and plurality voting systems alike. What was done without formal constitutional revision might be undone without it as well.

There is no point in having a representative legislature enact laws that can then be subverted in the process of implementation by civil servants hostile to the values of the legislators. To be complete, representative democracy requires representative bureaucracy.

In a modern administrative state, much de facto lawmaking will continue to be undertaken by administrative agencies; it is simply impossible for legislatures to identify and prescribe for all applications of a statute in advance. But even in the administrative state the power of the working class can be increased by assigning decision-making to independent agencies overseen by multimember commissions, at least some of whose members might have working-class constituents and affiliations, instead of centralized, insulated bureaucracies staffed at the highest levels by graduates of the Ivy League, Oxbridge, and the *grandes écoles*.

F INALLY, IN ADDITION to the need for countervailing power in the economy and politics there is a need for countervailing power to check the domination of the culture by the university-credentialed managerial elite. As the philosopher John Gray has observed, value pluralism is likely to be a permanent characteristic of modern democratic societies, so it is necessary to work out what he calls a "modus vivendi" among subcultures within the same country with profoundly different views of reality and morality—not only secularists and traditional religious believers but also believers in new supernatural or secular creeds.[7]

A value-pluralist modus vivendi is the opposite of the authoritarian imposition of the values of the ruling class on a religiously diverse population. Nineteenth-century Imperial Germany waged a *Kulturkampf* (culture war) on behalf of Protestantism against German Catholics. In the United States before World War II, mainline Protestants used the public schools to promulgate a generic Protestant religiosity in which the children of Catholics, Jews, and Protestant sectarians like Jehovah's Witnesses were compelled to participate. In France, the tradition of "laicity" inherited from the Jacobins of the French Revolution has similarly viewed the public school as a means of repressing religion and stripping subcultures of their particular identities.

Today religious and philosophical diversity are again under threat from the ruling classes of the transatlantic West.

For many members of the highly secularized university-educated overclass, premodern religious traditions and the secular Western Greco-Roman heritage have been replaced by ever-changing social science fashions, while clerical and humanist authorities have been replaced by academics, foundation-subsidized activists, and even corporate executives as the moral arbiters of society. "Corporations Are Replacing Churches as America's Conscience" was a headline in the neoliberal zine *Vox* in 2017.[8]

The evolution of managerialism in the West has replaced the distant and snobbish—but thankfully indifferent—bosses of the post-1945 years with a new "woke" corporate elite. Under the cross-class settlement in the mid-twentieth-century West, once the whistle blew, the proletarian could leave the factory gate for the safety of a world that excluded the bosses, a world of working-class neighborhoods, churches, clubs, and taverns. Under technocratic neoliberalism, however, the boss class pursues the working class after the workday has ended, trying to snatch the unhealthy steak or soda from the worker's plate, vilifying the theology of the worker's church as a firing offense and possibly an illegal hate crime to be reported to the police, and denouncing the racy, prole-oriented tabloid Internet as "fake news" to be censored by the guardians of neoliberal orthodoxy and propriety.

It is no wonder that the working classes of the Western democracies are rebelling against their arrogant and meddlesome overlords. As we have seen, one reason for the success of demagogic populist politicians in the US and Europe is their willingness to mock the pieties and flout the etiquette that the aggressive managerial overclass seeks to impose on working-class majorities from above.

In order to discourage overclass moral imperialism from provoking popular backlashes that can be exploited by populist false messiahs, the modus vivendi in a democratic pluralist society must guarantee coexistence among different creeds and subcultures. In the United States, the threat to pluralism from the religious right, represented by the Moral Majority and the Christian Coalition, which sought to legislate sectarian values into law, has been thwarted and is unlikely to return. Moreover, religious affiliation in the United States is declining to the low levels long found in Europe.

But churches, synagogues, and mosques are among the last remaining influential nonprofit institutions that are not funded and controlled by donors and foundation program officers with identical social views who reside in a few major hub cities. And religious institutions that are distasteful or threatening to the secular managerial ruling class are likely to be important in any vigorous and authentic working-class politics.

Creedal congregations should be defined broadly, to include secular groups like American Atheists and neo-pagan creeds like Wiccans, who according to some reports now outnumber Presbyterians in the United States.[9] Whether its belief system is secular or supernatural, each creedal congregation must have the legal right to organize and govern itself internally on the basis of its own beliefs and traditions, regardless of whether these offend modern technocratic neoliberal ideals. Tax laws should be more generous to creedal congregations that raise their money from their own members than to nonprofit organizations that raise funding from the rich and from donor foundations endowed by the rich.

At the same time, provision must be made for creedal congregations to defend themselves by taking part in public policy making that affects their missions. For example, legislation should require the participation of a representative range of secular and supernaturalist creedal groups in government boards and commissions that oversee media policy and education policy to ensure that the values of all major subcultures in the nation are acknowledged and given deference. Today in the US it would be unthinkable for a civil rights commission to have no African American or Latino members. It should be equally unthinkable for a commission or agency that makes rules for the media, public school curricula, or college accreditation to include no devout Catholics, Protestants, Jews, Muslims, and members of other major religious or secular creeds.

Restoring the countervailing power of the multiracial, religiously diverse working-class majorities in Western democracies means defying familiar categories of right and left. Today it may mean defending the institutional independence of religious communities and tomorrow the promotion of pragmatic municipal socialism. Institutions capable of aggregating the collective power of working-class citizens in the twenty-first century would resemble historic precedents like the Salvation Army and old-fashioned Milwaukee-style "sewer socialism" (municipal ownership of public utilities), rather than the social justice and climate change NGOs funded by billionaires and run by progressive overclass professionals or, for that matter, the free market agitprop groups funded by the libertarian rich.

Like their working-class constituents, contemporary membership-based movements would mix sentimental patriotism with economic egalitarianism and religious communalism with support for social insurance entitlements and free public goods. They would probably combine crude demotic speech and civic rhetoric in ways quite alien to managerial-class conservatives, centrists, and progressives alike. In the best sense, they would be vulgar.

CHAPTER NINE

Making the World Safe for Democratic Pluralism

FOLLOWING THE COLD WAR, neoliberals in the US and Europe promoted a vision of a new world order that was liberal and democratic. Unfortunately, that vision included a lot of liberalism and very little democracy.

As we have seen, technocratic neoliberal elites sought to drain democratic national governments and elected legislatures of authority, even as the Clinton, Bush, and Obama administrations sought to spread democracy by bombing and invading countries with undemocratic regimes from the Balkans to the Middle East and Central Asia. In newly liberated countries, citizens could vote, but the new democracy like the old ones was limited in its sovereignty in the economic realm by transnational trade and investment treaties and bodies like the World Trade Organization. At the same time, champions of "the right to protect" and "humanitarian intervention" made state sovereignty conditioned on the willingness of governments to conform to Western notions of civil liberties, violation of which could justify the US and its allies in toppling a regime, invading the country, and occupying it for years or decades.

The democratic pluralist vision of a democratic world order is quite different from the technocratic neoliberal vision, with its powerful transnational rules combined with weak nation-states and legislatures.

For democratic pluralists, free and fair elections are a necessary but not sufficient condition for genuine democracy. A country run by an aristocracy or oligarchy is a democracy in name only, even if citizens are free to vote for competing aristocratic or oligarchic factions. According to democratic pluralism, electoral democracy in the political realm, narrowly defined, must be accompanied by power-sharing arrangements among classes and subcultures in the realms of the economy and the culture. These power-sharing institutions, like tripartite labor-business-government wage-setting institutions, need not resemble one-person, one-vote political democracy. But there must be social checks and balances in addition to political checks and balances. And decisions should be based as much as possible on hard-won and lasting consensus among negotiating parties, classes and creeds, not on fluctuating numerical majorities.

The democratic pluralist version of democracy necessarily puts great emphasis on national sovereignty—external sovereignty, not internal sovereignty. All of the various schools of thought that inform the democratic pluralist tradition— English pluralists, French solidarists, Catholic corporatists, and New Deal defenders of countervailing power in the broker state—reject the eighteenth-century idea of unlimited popular sovereignty shared by the American and French revolutions.

For democratic pluralists, the state—usually a nation-state, but sometimes a multinational state or independent city-state—is not a mass of individuals to whom a general will can be attributed, but a community made up of smaller communities.

But while democratic pluralism rejects the idea of the unlimited internal sovereignty of any group, including "the People" as a whole, external sovereignty is indispensable. The reason is that the negotiations and compromises among communities that are the essence of democratic pluralism can only occur within the fixed boundaries of a political community with fixed membership. Cross-class compromises among labor and business, for example, are pointless if businesses can unilaterally annul the contracts at any time by transferring operations to foreign workers or bringing foreign workers into the country to weaken or replace organized labor. The various cross-class settlements in the US and Europe from the 1940s to the 1970s would not have been possible if employers had been able to use large-scale tax and regulatory arbitrage and offshoring and access to high amounts of low-wage, non-union immigrant labor to escape the constraints imposed on them by "new deals" with organized labor and democratic national governments.

For this reason, a world order that can support many countries organized along democratic pluralist lines will be quite different from a neoliberal world order in which most decision-making has been transferred from nation-states to supranational institutions or from national legislatures to national executive bureaucracies and judiciaries. Rejecting neoliberalism at the national level requires the rejection of neoliberalism at the global level as well. A world safe for democratic pluralism will not be a neoliberal world order.

THE ECONOMIST DANI RODRIK has argued that "democracy, national sovereignty and global economic integration are mutually incompatible: we can combine any two of the three, but never have all three simultaneously and in full."[1] If Rodrik's trilemma, or "impossibility theorem," is correct, then global integration should be sacrificed to the need to preserve and strengthen the peace treaty among the classes at home.

At the global level, this requires abandoning the ideal of a rule-governed global market for an à la carte approach to cross-border integration. Rich and poor countries alike should be allowed to use national developmentalist strategies tailored to their particular needs.[2]

The term "developmental state" was used by scholars like Chalmers Johnson, Alice Amsden, and Meredith Woo-Cumings to describe the post-1945 regimes of Japan, South Korea, Taiwan, and Singapore, which relied on export-oriented strategies as part of programs to industrialize and catch up with the West.[3] But as the economists Erik Reinert, Ha-Joon Chang, and Michael Hudson, among others, have demonstrated, the mercantilism of Renaissance and early modern Western city-states, kingdoms, and empires was a version of developmentalism.[4] Britain before the 1840s, Imperial Germany, the US before World War II (and to some degree to this day), Gaullist France, Japan, South Korea, Taiwan, and China have all had state-sponsored systems of national industrial development and technological innovation.

National economic development has two goals—widespread

national productivity and widely shared national prosperity. Productivity growth must be encouraged in all sectors, not just a few advanced industries that glitter in a morass of stagnation. And the gains from growth must be shared among the managerial overclass and the working-class majority.

The two goals—productivity and prosperity—cannot be separated. If productivity is increased but the gains are concentrated in a tiny oligarchy, the country will lack a mass home market of consumers as an adequate base for globally competitive industries with increasing returns to scale, something that remains important in our less-than-global economy. The country will have temporarily purchased national productivity at the price of class peace. If, by means of redistribution, incomes are equalized but productivity stagnates or declines, the country will fall further and further behind more productive foreign rivals. The country will have temporarily purchased class peace at the price of national productivity.

In the system that succeeds today's neoliberalism, global integration should be subordinated to the need to preserve and strengthen the democratic pluralist peace treaty among the managerial class and the working class at home, while government, business, and organized labor work together to promote technological modernization and shared gains from growth. The neoliberal argument that governments must not interfere in globalization, and can therefore only compensate the losers or help them to adapt, must be rejected. It is not necessary to reject trade and immigration as such. But democratic nation-states can, and should, engage in selective globalization. They should adopt strategic trade policies and selective immigration policies in the interest of national productivity, national solidarity, and the bargaining power of citizen-workers and legal immigrants in negotiations with employers.

Compared to the devastation of industrial workers and industrial regions in the US and Europe that has contributed to the rise of antisystem populism, the benefits to consumers from imports from low-wage countries have been trivial, as even some defenders of offshoring admit. A 2017 report prepared for the US-China Business Council for Oxford Economics estimated that "average prices are 1–1.5 percent lower as a result of imports from China. Oxford Economics estimates the influence of such low prices boosted US GDP by up to 0.8 percent in 2015." Oxford Economics cites other studies that have concluded "that greater import penetration from China reduced US inflation by about 0.1 percent annually in the late 1990s and early 2000s" and that an Apple iPhone might cost 5 percent more if assembled in the US.[5]

Does the benefit to workers in developing countries outweigh the cost to developed-country workers of cheap-labor globalization? When China is excluded from the data, developing countries grew at a lower rate in the globalizing era of 1980–2000 than in the more protectionist period of 1960–1980.[6] Dani Rodrik has argued that developing countries today and in the future can no longer benefit from export-oriented manufacturing strategies like those of China, Japan, South Korea, and Taiwan and must instead focus on upgrading their nontraded domestic service industries.[7]

GLOBAL LABOR ARBITRAGE in the forms of offshoring and immigration is not the only cause of rising inequality and stagnant wages in the US and similar nations, or even the most important. Only a minority of workers labor in import-competing industries or compete directly against immigrants at home. And wages and unemployment levels are affected by many other factors, including changes in tax laws, reclassification of employees as independent contractors, zero-hours contracts, central bank austerity policies, and, in the US, the continuing practice of interregional labor arbitrage among states and the erosion of the minimum wage by inflation. But the two forms of global labor arbitrage have had their effects multiplied by weakening two institutions that reinforce the bargaining power of workers: unions and the welfare state.

Private sector labor unions managed to limit the arbitrary power of employers from World War II until late in the Cold War.[8] Union membership in the US has plummeted from roughly a third in the mid-twentieth century to only 10.5 percent in 2018.[9] This is a transatlantic trend. While a few countries retain high union density, among the developed nations of the Organization for Economic Cooperation and Development (OECD), the percentage of the labor force that is unionized has declined from 30 percent to 17 percent on average.[10]

This matters because, according to one estimate, the decline in unionization explains as much as a third of the growth in wage inequality.[11] The link between coverage by collective bargaining agreements and the share of the working poor in Western nations is indisputable. In the US, with only one in ten workers covered by union contracts, more than a quarter work in low-wage jobs. In France and Denmark, where more than 80 percent of workers are covered, only 11 and 8 percent, respectively, receive low wages.[12]

Labor unions can be weakened or destroyed by offshoring or the threat of offshoring, or in some cases by the use of immigrants, legal or illegal, as a reserve army of labor. In the case of automobile unions, the effects of labor arbitrage—both within nations and among them—are obvious. Not only American firms but also German, Japanese, and South Korean car companies have avoided dealing with unionized workforces in the American "rust belt" by moving jobs to nonunion workforces in the American South and Mexico.[13] The use by employers of immigrants, both legal and illegal, to weaken or destroy unions in US sectors like agriculture and meatpacking and janitorial work has been well documented.[14]

The mere threat of replacement by foreign workers or immigrants can serve to intimidate a much larger group than those who are actually replaced. During the economic boom of the 1990s more than half of all employers in one study, to discourage union organizing, threatened to shut down all or part of a plant, even though employers acted on the threat in fewer than 3 percent of the cases.[15]

IN ADDITION TO weakening organized labor, high levels of immigration can reduce public support for welfare state services that bolster the bargaining power of workers by allowing them to "hold out" longer in negotiations with employers. In modern Western welfare states, lower-paid immigrant workers may compete with better-paid native workers for limited public resources such as schools, hospitals, welfare services, or, in some countries, public housing. Even in the absence of direct occupational rivalry, this competition for public goods among ethnically divided sections of the working class can provoke a backlash that is channeled against the welfare state itself.

The incompatibility of the welfare state with mass immigration was noted by the libertarian economist Milton Friedman: "If you have a welfare state, if you have a state in which every resident is promised a certain minimum level of income, or a minimum level of subsistence, regardless of whether he works or not, produces it or not. Then [free immigration] really is an impossible thing." Friedman callously welcomed illegal immigration—but only as long as illegal immigrants were ineligible for welfare: "But it's only good so long as it's illegal. . . . Make it legal and it's no good. Why? Because as long as it's illegal the people who come in do not qualify for welfare, they don't qualify for social security, they don't qualify for the other myriad of benefits."[16]

His ideological opposite, the progressive economist Paul Krugman, agrees with Friedman's political point. Because "modern America is a welfare state" and "low-skill immigrants don't pay enough taxes to cover the cost of the benefits they receive," Krugman observes that the "political threat that low-skill immigration poses to the welfare state is more serious" than its other consequences.[17]

The new open-borders left might reply that unlimited immigration would not be a problem if all workers in a country were unionized, including immigrants who joined unions on arrival. In addition, the open-borders left could speculate that voters who were not racist or otherwise bigoted against particular groups of immigrants for noneconomic reasons would not begrudge the use of the welfare system by wave after wave of poor people from other nations.

Perhaps the open-borders left is correct. But shouldn't such a radical proposition be tested first in one or two countries, before other democratic nations take a chance on it? Let a small democratic nation-state known for the antiracist attitudes of its population, its high levels of unionization and its generous welfare state adopt an open borders policy, allowing anyone on the planet to move there and immediately use welfare benefits on the same terms as citizens, without having previously paid into the system through taxes and with no waiting period for eligibility. After a generation or two, the results of the experiment of a highly unionized welfare state with an open borders immigration policy can be examined—assuming, of course, that the experiment does not quickly trigger an anti-immigration revolt that brings demagogic populists to power and the experiment in open-borders leftism to a swift and unpleasant stop.

IF A NEW democratic pluralism were to bring the new class war to an end with a new class peace based on cross-class power sharing, then a chief goal of immigration policy would be to strengthen the bargaining power of national workers with employers. As long as the bargaining power of workers relative to that of employers was not undermined, some democratic nation-states in some circumstances might choose higher levels of legal immigration, including less-skilled immigration.

The arguments that are typically made for high levels of less-skilled immigration, however, are surprisingly weak. For example, it is often asserted that there are many menial jobs that citizens of the United States and European countries refuse to do.

This is a common theme among rich people who feel entitled to a supporting cast of low-wage, foreign-born servants. The billionaire and former New York mayor Michael Bloomberg has asked: "Who takes care of the greens and the fairways in your golf courses?"[18] Speaking to a wealthy audience in Abu Dhabi, at a summit organized by the disgraced former financier Michael Milken's think tank, former president George W. Bush, the former governor of Texas, once the leading cotton-producing slave state in the US, declared: "Americans don't want to pick cotton at 105 degrees but there are people who want to put food on their family's tables and are willing to do that."[19] Another Texan born like Bush into an upper-class family, Representative Robert "Beto" O'Rourke, agreed with Bush, his partisan and political opposite, that low-wage immigrants were needed to pick and process cotton in the former Confederate state of Texas. When an African American Texan asked O'Rourke about illegal immigrants, the West Texas patrician uncritically quoted the owner of a cotton gin: "[T]here are twenty-four jobs and the manager of that gin says it does not matter the wages that I pay or the number of hours that we set, there is no one born in Roscoe . . . or Texas or this country who is willing to work."[20]

History records no instance in which all of a country's cotton pickers, groundskeepers, maids, or construction workers abruptly decided they were too good for the job and quit the industry en masse. The domination of particular occupations by immigrants instead of native workers typically results from an earlier prolonged period of discrimination by employers who prefer immigrants willing to work for less and afraid to complain. In the United States, this phenomenon is evident in the construction and meatpacking sectors, among other industries.[21]

Robert Shapiro argued in 2019 that much of the unexpected contraction in employment among native white Americans in recent years had been the result of direct competition of white workers who shared higher wage expectations with immigrants as well as members of minority groups willing to work for lower wages:

> A final critical reason why many employers are more inclined to hire Hispanics, Asians, and blacks than whites in this business cycle is the economics of wages. At every educational level, except people without high school degrees, whites' wages are higher than the wages of blacks, Hispanics and, in some cases, Asians. There is a long history of immigrants and minorities working for less than others with the same education, sometimes willingly and often unwillingly. Italians, Poles, Eastern Europeans, and Irish, as well as blacks, did so a century ago. Apparently, that pattern has not changed a great deal.[22]

Coming from any other source, this acknowledgment that many American employers are indeed using immigrants in labor arbitrage strategies to undercut wage levels would have been denounced by the new open-borders left as "Trumpist" nativism or racism, scapegoating immigrants for employment problems that allegedly have unrelated causes like automation or a lack of skills. But the author was a senior adviser to Hillary Clinton's presidential campaign, President Bill Clinton's principal economic adviser in 1991–92, and later Clinton's undersecretary of commerce for economic affairs. Even more striking, Shapiro's essay was published in the flagship journal of the American intellectual center-left, *Democracy Journal*. Coming from a pillar of the neoliberal establishment, in a publication long identified with neoliberalism, this is a remarkably candid admission.

If there really were shortages of farmworkers and janitors, rather than merely a preference by employers for hiring easily-intimidated immigrants willing to work for little, then wages in those sectors would be shooting up. Rather than attract applicants by raising wages, these entitled employers demand an in-kind labor subsidy from the government in the form of policies importing low-wage immigrants, preferably indentured-servant guest workers who cannot vote or unionize.

If employers had to raise wages to attract workers to unattractive jobs, inventors, investors and entrepreneurs would have an incentive to invest in automation to substitute technology for more-expensive labor. Another alternative would be self-help. Writing in the *New York Times*, Patricia Cohen notes that "many tasks that most people previously did themselves—mowing lawns, polishing nails, picking up takeout, driving—are now contracted out because there is labor to do them."[23]

Opposing the self-help option, the neoliberal journalist Matthew Yglesias has argued that low-wage immigration is good because it provides college-educated professionals with inexpensive maids:

But it's obvious that in a world without immigrant housecleaners, we wouldn't have an equal number of much-higher-paid native-born maids. What we'd have is less housecleaning done on a market basis and more being done as unpaid work at home. For many middle-class families that would be pure waste. Time spent cleaning the toilet that could be spent on higher-value labor, on leisure, or on quality time with friends and family.[24]

A more serious argument for mass unskilled immigration than the danger that maid shortages will inconvenience the overclass involves economic growth. The claim that immigration expands the national economy as a whole is true but trivial; increasing any country's workforce by any means, including the abolition of retirement, the abandonment of wages and hours laws, and the legalization of child labor, would increase a country's overall GDP by definition.

What counts are the distributional effects of mass unskilled immigration and these differ among races as well as among classes. The beneficiaries tend to be affluent overclass households that hire servants and firms whose business models rely on cheap labor. The victims are the working poor, including previous waves of immigrant workers. According to the US Commission on Civil Rights in 2010, "illegal immigration to the United States in recent decades has tended to depress both wages and employment rates for low-skilled American citizens, a disproportionate number of whom are black men."[25] A 2017 National Academies of Sciences, Engineering, and Medicine report noted that previous studies had found "more-negative results for low-education black's than low-education whites" and "larger negative effects for Hispanic dropouts than for all dropouts. This could be because native dropout minorities are the closest native substitutes for immigrants."[26]

A related argument attributes a magical economic multiplier effect to immigrants. To lobby for more H-1B guest worker visas for foreign nationals, who are legally bound as indentured servants to their sponsoring corporations or intermediary firms known as "body shops," Facebook's Mark Zuckerberg and other Silicon Valley executives have formed a lobbying group named FWD.us. In the *Washington Post* Zuckerberg wrote: "Why do we offer so few H1B visas for talented specialists that the supply runs out within days of becoming available each year, even though we know each of these jobs will create two or three more American jobs in return?"[27]

The claim that each foreign indentured servant admitted under the H-1B nonimmigrant visa program has a Midas touch capable of creating two to three American jobs is ridiculous. If it were true, importing 50 million H-1B guest workers all at once could create up to 150 million jobs in the US overnight—the equivalent of the entire US workforce.

A legitimate case can be made for modestly increasing skilled immigration. As we have seen, there is widespread public support in Western democracies for increasing the numbers of skilled immigrants, even among many who want unskilled immigration to be cut. But if their numbers are increased, skilled immigrants should be legal permanent residents with the rights to quickly become citizens and to quit one employer for another, not easily intimidated and easily exploited indentured servants whose lack of bargaining power makes them attractive substitutes for workers who possess more rights.

A NOTHER FALLACIOUS ARGUMENT holds that it will be necessary in the future for aging countries with low fertility rates like those of Europe and North America to import enormous numbers of immigrants to maintain the "dependency ratio"—the ratio of workers to retirees and other dependents, including children. This argument is intuitively plausible—and dead wrong.

How many immigrants would be needed to maintain today's dependency ratio in the US indefinitely? In 2000, the UN Population Division calculated that in order to maintain the worker-to-retiree ratio in the US, the US would have to increase legal immigration from roughly 1 million a year to 12 million a year, adding more than half a billion additional net immigrants to the US population by 2050.[28] Using more recent data, the Center for Immigration Studies has estimated that maintaining the US worker-to-retiree ratio would require increasing immigration fivefold, more than doubling the US population between now and 2060, to 706 million.[29] Even worse, in order to maintain a fixed dependency ratio of workers to an ever-growing number of retirees, the US would need to import ever-growing numbers of immigrants until the unsustainable demographic Ponzi scheme collapsed when the rest of the world was depopulated.

Those who claim that mass immigration is needed to maintain dependency ratios in Western nations exaggerate the change in those ratios caused by population aging. Under a scenario in which US immigration was slashed by two-thirds to stabilize the population, in 2060 there would be 2.2 workers per retiree, compared to 2.5 workers in an alternate scenario in which the US adds 46 million net immigrants by 2060.[30] This is hardly a crisis.

Fortunately, the challenges posed to social insurance systems in the West can be solved in ways that do not require North America and Europe rapidly to import immigrants until they are more populous than China and India—or, for that matter, to try to boost native fertility to balloon their populations to gargantuan dimensions. The rational methods to ensure the fiscal sustainability of social insurance entitlements are growth in productivity per worker, revenues other than payroll taxes, higher taxes or cuts in benefits. In the words of the US Census Bureau's Population Projection branch: "International migration may address a high dependency ratio decisively in the short term, yet is highly inefficient in reducing it over the long term—especially if considerations of population scale, as well as age composition, are taken into account."[31]

THE AMOUNT AND composition of immigration that is best for one country may not be best for another. But certain principles should guide immigration policy in any nation organized on the basis of democratic pluralism. A pro-labor immigration policy would seek to minimize split labor markets which can be gamed by employers who can pick and choose among different categories of workers with different legal rights.

The most fundamental labor right is the right to quit a job and find another, without needing to leave the country. For this reason, indentured servitude in the form of guest worker programs, which bind a worker to a single employer as a condition for working in a country, is a political abomination. Guest worker programs threaten all workers in the sectors in which they are permitted by allowing employers to hire bound serfs instead of workers who can respond to mistreatment or low pay by quitting. For this reason, all or most temporary guest worker programs that allow employers to hire foreign nationals as indentured servants should be abolished. If foreign nationals, other than a tiny number of foreign orchestra conductors and visiting professors, are allowed to work at all in a country, they should have the status described in the US as "legal permanent residents" (green card holders).

To further thwart divide-and-rule schemes by employers, all working-age immigrants should have rights that are identical to those of native and naturalized workers, including the right to take part in collective bargaining and the right to rely on the national safety net on equal terms. Rather than deny welfare-state benefits to low-wage workers, it is better not to import low-wage workers.

The sole exception to identical rights for citizen-workers and legal immigrants should be the right to vote. And to minimize the existence of substantial numbers of workers who are not citizens and cannot vote, the naturalization of immigrants who seek to become citizens should take place in as brief a period as possible. To this end, in 2007 in the *New York Times* I proposed reducing the waiting period for legal immigrants to become citizens of the US from five years to two years.[32] Better yet, legal immigrants should be allowed to vote as soon as they have applied for citizenship.

Denying employers the ability to pit different groups of workers against one another also makes it necessary to enact amnesties for illegal immigrants in countries like the US where large numbers of unauthorized foreign nationals, allowed to settle in the country by corrupt politicians in the interest of economic elites, are de facto citizens. Rewarding foreign nationals for violating immigration laws is an evil. But it is the lesser of two evils, compared to allowing employers to have continuing access to large pools of illegal immigrant workers who can be mistreated and intimidated. Like legal immigrants, amnestied illegal immigrants without criminal records should be made citizens as rapidly as possible to deny employers access to workers who cannot vote. Needless to say, the purpose of an amnesty in denying firms and households access to a split labor market would be thwarted, if future illegal immigration were not adequately deterred, chiefly by reducing the demand for it by means of severe penalties on law-breaking employers.

As John B. Judis has observed, "Without national control over multinational corporations and banks and without control of borders and immigration, it is very hard to imagine the United States becoming a more egalitarian society. . . . Globalization is incompatible with social democracy in Europe or with New Deal liberalism in the United States."[33] The national economy should serve the national working-class majority, and the global economy should serve national economies. Every democratic nation-state should tailor both its immigration policy and its trade policy to promote the interests of the members of its working-class majority, native-born and foreign-born alike. In the era that succeeds neoliberalism, the "four freedoms" of neoliberalism—freedom of movement for people, goods, services, and capital—should be replaced by the "four regulations."

Epilogue

TECHNOCRATIC NEOLIBERALISM has been the governing philosophy of the Western democracies since the late twentieth century. But it is not the natural or inevitable ideology of the managerial elite. On the contrary, modern managerial elites in different countries and in different eras have governed on the basis of various ideologies—democratic pluralism in New Deal America and postwar Western Europe, neoliberalism in the West from Reagan and Thatcher to Obama and Macron, National Socialism in Hitler's Germany, Marxism-Leninism in the Soviet Union and the People's Republic of China.

It is not necessary for the managerial overclasses of Western nations to be overthrown in order for technocratic neoliberalism to be defeated. It is only necessary for existing Western managerial elites to abandon technocratic neoliberalism for a different governing philosophy—preferably one that is better, like a new democratic pluralism, rather than one that is as bad or worse. Most members of the elite under the new policy regime will have been members of the elite under the old one. The fact that most ruling classes include large numbers of opportunistic careerists is a blessing in disguise. It means that a radical revolution in policy can take place, without a radical replacement of personnel.

What would motivate the managerial overclass to abandon technocratic neoliberalism? The answer is fear. History demonstrates that ruling classes of any kind are reluctant to share power with the ruled unless they are afraid of the ruled or afraid of rival countries.

Fear of the ruled is a weak motive. Popular revolts seldom turn into revolutions, unless the rebels are supported by dissident members of the ruling class or a foreign elite, like the French monarchy that bankrolled and supported US independence from Britain for its own purposes.

Fear of national defeat in war— hot war, cold war, or trade war—is more likely to compel elites to undertake reforms than fear of uprisings from below. In the twentieth century, the need to promote business-labor collaboration and cross-class harmony and to reduce racial strife in the world wars and the Cold War overcame the natural resistance of Western elites to sharing power, if only briefly, with organized labor.

If today's technocratic neoliberalism is succeeded in the future by a new democratic pluralism, it is likely to be in the context of renewed great-power competition. In order to compete effectively with rival powers, patriotic factions within the overclass who put long-term national solidarity and national productivity above the short-term self-interest of their class may lead to the replacement of globalist neoliberalism with a new national developmentalism, combined with cross-class negotiations in the interest of social peace on the home front.

The experience of contemporary East Asian democracies—Japan, South Korea, and Taiwan—proves that neoliberalism is not the only model for a high-tech modern democracy. In comparison with the US and Europe, these nations admit few immigrants and have offshored industrial production to a far lesser degree. Unlike in the West, there has been no radical elite-imposed rupture in their social systems between the mid-twentieth century and the present. As a result, although they have populist politicians now and then, and suffer from other problems, including low birthrates, they have experienced nothing like the populist rebellion against neoliberalism that is shattering political systems in Europe and North America.

In a contest between the economic model represented in different ways by Japan, South Korea, and Taiwan, minus their traditional export-oriented mercantilism, on the one hand, and, on the other hand, the rentier-dominated oligarchic model represented by Brazil and Mexico, it would be foolish to wager on the latter. North American and European democracies cannot and should not emulate modern East Asian developmental states in every detail. Still, it should be a cause for concern that, since the Cold War, the United States and Western Europe have been moving along the spectrum, as it were, away from East Asia toward Latin America.

MANAGERIAL ELITES ARE destined to dominate the economy and society of every modern nation. But if they are not checked, they will overreach and produce a destructive populist backlash in proportion to their excess.

If there is not to be perpetual conflict among the two permanent classes of technological society, the new class war must come to an end in one of two ways.

One possibility is that there will be a new cross-class compromise embodied in a new democratic pluralist order, providing the working-class majorities in Western nations with far greater countervailing power in politics, the economy, and the culture than they possess today.

The alternative—the triumph of one class over the other, be it the overclass led by neoliberal technocrats or the working class led by populist demagogues—would be calamitous. A West dominated by technocratic neoliberalism would be a high-tech caste society. A West dominated by demagogic populism would be stagnant and corrupt.

Given the weakness and disorganization of national working classes, in the absence of a new democratic pluralism the most likely possibility is that today's class war will come to an end when, in one Western country after another, the managerial minority, with its near monopoly of wealth, political power, expertise, media influence, and academic authority, completely and successfully represses the numerically greater but politically weaker working-class majority.

If that should occur, the future of North America and Europe may look a lot like the present of Brazil and Mexico, with nepotistic oligarchies clustered in a few swollen metropolitan areas surrounded by hinterlands that are derelict, depopulated, and despised. What Fritz Lang's *Metropolis* (1927), with its managers in skyscrapers and its oppressed factory workers underground, was for an earlier industrial era, Neill Blomkamp's *Elysium* (2013), with its sybaritic elite in orbit and its desperate earthbound slum-dwellers, might prove to be for the era that succeeds neoliberalism—a prophecy in the form of a nightmare.

Only power can check power. Only a major reassertion of the political power, economic leverage, and cultural influence of national wage-earning majorities of all races, ethnicities, and creeds can stop the degeneration of the US and other Western democracies into high-tech banana republics. To supplement conventional electoral politics, reformers will need to rebuild old institutions or build new ones that can integrate working-class citizens of all origins into decision-making in government, the economy, and the culture, so that everyone can be an insider.

Reconstructing democratic pluralism in North America and Europe to permit cross-class power sharing is a challenge as difficult as it is urgent. The alternative is grim: a future of gated communities and mobs led by demagogues at their gates.

Acknowledgments

Twenty-five years ago in my first book, *The Next American Nation*, I described the growing consolidation of political power, economic control, and cultural authority by the managerial overclass. Events and trends since 1995 in the United States and Europe have vindicated most of my analysis. Following three decades in which I lived and worked in Washington, DC, and New York City, I have grown pessimistic that overclass domination can be checked by conventional electoral democracy, unless it is supplemented by the kind of cross-class power-sharing institutions I describe in this book under the name of democratic pluralism.

The New Class War is based on two essays in *American Affairs*. I would like to thank its editors, Julius Krein and Gladden Pappen, as well as the editors of *The Breakthrough Journal* and *National Review*, where some of the material in this book originally appeared.

I am grateful to Dean Angela Evans of the Lyndon B. Johnson School of Public Affairs of the University of Texas at Austin for giving me the opportunity to serve as a professor at my alma mater in my home town. I owe thanks to Anne-Marie Slaughter, CEO of New America, for allowing me to continue my relationship with New America, the think tank I cofounded, as a fellow.

I'm deeply indebted to Bria Sandford, my editor at Portfolio, and to my agent, Kristine Dahl, of International Creative Management.

Limited space prevents me from listing all of those who have influenced my thinking on the topics in this book. Among contemporary scholars, who may reject some or all of my arguments and conclusions, I would like to acknowledge intellectual debts to Julius Krein on managerialism; David Marquand on pluralism; Edna Bonacich on split labor markets; Theda Skocpol on mass-membership organizations; Sheri Berman and Wolfgang Streeck on the history of social democracy; David Goodhart, Eric Kaufmann, Matthew Goodwin, Christophe Guilluy, and Nancy Fraser on populism, nationalism, and social class; Yascha Mounk on undemocratic liberalism; James K. Galbraith, Robert D. Atkinson, Dani Rodrik, Erik Reinert, Ha-Joon Chang, and Robert Kuttner on the economy; Daniel McCarthy on palliative liberalism; Reihan Salam, the late Vernon M. Briggs, and the late Richard Estrada on immigration; and Lee Drutman, Ruy Texeira, and Thomas B. Edsall on electoral coalitions.

I have benefited over many years from reading and conversing with Sherle Schwenninger, Walter Russell Mead, Joel Kotkin, John Gray, Roberto Unger, Emmanuel Todd, and Marshall Auerback. And I am especially indebted to John B. Judis, with whom I have discussed and debated the subjects of nationalism and democracy for a quarter of a century. Their views, as well, may differ from mine.

Finally, I would like to pay tribute to Ernesto Cortes Jr., whose life's work proves that countervailing power is more than a phrase.

Notes

INTRODUCTION

1. Jacob Funk Kirkegaard, "Macron's Victory Signals Reform in France and a Stronger Europe," PIIE, May 8, 2017.
2. Will Marshall, "How Emmanuel Macron Became the New Leader of the Free World," *Politico*, April 22, 2018.
3. For good overviews of the rise of populist parties and movements, see John B. Judis, *The Nationalist Revival: Trade, Immigration, and the Revolt Against Globalization* (New York: Columbia Global Reports, 2018) and *The Populist Explosion* (New York: Columbia Global Reports, 2016); Roger Eatwell and Matthew Goodwin, *National Populism: The Revolt Against Liberal Democracy* (New York: Pelican, 2018); Christophe Guilluy, *Twilight of the Elites: Prosperity, the Periphery, and the Future of France* (New Haven, CT: Yale University Press, 2019).
4. Rakib Ehsan, "Many Ethnic-Minority Voters Backed Brexit, Too," *Spiked*, March 26, 2019; Harry Enten, "Trump Probably Did Better With Latino Voters Than Romney Did," FiveThirtyEight, November 18, 2016.

CHAPTER ONE: THE NEW CLASS WAR

1. Julius Krein, "James Burnham's Managerial Elite," *American Affairs* 1, no. 1, Spring 2017; Matthew Continetti, "The Managers vs. the Managed," *Weekly Standard*, September 21, 2015.

2. John Kenneth Galbraith, *American Capitalism: The Concept of Countervailing Power* (Boston: Houghton Mifflin, 1952). According to Galbraith, the power of big business could be offset by large purchasers, cooperatives, chain stores, farmers' associations, and labor unions: "The operation of countervailing power is to be seen with the greatest clarity in the labor market, where it is also most fully developed (p. 121).

3. Adolf A Berle Jr. and Gardiner C. Means, *The Modern Corporation and Private Property* (New York: Macmillan, 1932); Bruno Rizzi, *The Bureaucratization of the World*, trans. Adam Westoby (New York: Free Press, 1985 [1939]).

4. James Burnham, *The Managerial Revolution: What Is Happening in the World* (Westport, CT: Greenwood Press, 1972 [1941]), p. 72.

5. George Orwell, "Second Thoughts on James Burnham," *Polemic*, May 1946.

6. John Kenneth Galbraith, *A Life in Our Times* (Boston: Houghton Mifflin Harcourt, 1981), p. 362.

7. Thorstein Veblen, *The Engineers and the Price System* (New York: B. W. Huebsch, 1921), chapter vi, "A Memorandum on a Practicable Soviet of Technicians," pp. 138–69.

8. Mark Bovens and Anchrit Wille, *Diploma Democracy: The Rise of Political Meritocracy* (New York: Oxford University Press, 2017), p. 5.

9. Matthew Stewart, "The 9.9 Percent Is the New American Aristocracy," *Atlantic*, June 2018.

10. Emily Forrest Cataldi, Christopher T. Bennett, and Xiangei Chen, "First-Generation Students: College Access, Persistence, and Postbachelor's Outcomes," National Center for Education Statistics, U.S. Department of Education, February 2018. See also Grace Bird, "The Impact of Parents' Educational Levels," *Inside Higher Ed*, February 8, 2018; Ronald Brownstein, "Are College Degrees Inherited?" *Atlantic*, April 11, 2014; Richard V. Reeves, "Dream Stealers: How Entrance into Elite US Colleges Is Rigged in Every Way," Brookings Institution op ed, March 13, 2019; Richard V. Reeves, "Dream Hoarders: How the American Upper Middle Class Is Leaving Everyone Else in

the Dust, Why That Is a Problem, and What to Do About It" (Washington, DC: Brookings Institution Press, 2017). For Europe, see Ludger Woessmann, "How Equal Are Educational Opportunities? Family Background and Student Achievement in Europe and the United States," Discussion Paper No. 1284 (Bonn, Germany: Institute for the Study of Labor [IZA], September 2004); OECD (2014), "Indicator A4: To What Extent Does Parents' Education Influence Participation in Tertiary Education?" in *Education at a Glance 2014: OECD Indicators* (OECD Publishing); Katherine Baird, "Where Do Youth Follow in Their Parents' Footsteps?" Presented in Session 4.2, "Parents-Offspring Relations and Life Satisfaction," at the Third International European Social Survey Conference Lausanne, Switzerland, July 13–16, 2016.

11. Julia B. Isaacs, "International Comparisons of Economic Mobility," in Julia B. Isaacs, Isabel V. Sawhill, and Ron Haskins, *Getting Ahead or Losing Ground: Economic Mobility in America* (Washington, DC: Brookings Institution, February 20, 2008), pp. 38–39.

12. Gregory Clark and Neil Cummins, "Surnames and Social Mobility" and "Intergenerational Mobility in England, 1858–2012. Wealth, Surnames, and Social Mobility," accessed via "England's Social Classes Slow to Evolve," www.lse.ac.uk, October 29, 2013. Their research was included in Clark and Cummins, *The Son Also Rises: Surnames and the History of Social Mobility* (Princeton, NJ: Princeton University Press, 2014).

13. Anthony P. Carnevale, Megan L. Fasules, Michael C. Quinn, and Kathryn Peltier Campbell, *Born to Win, Schooled to Lose: Why Talented Students Don't Get Equal Chances to Be All They Can Be*, Georgetown University Center on Education and the Workforce report, 2019.

14. UNCTAD, "Annex Table 24. The World's Top 100 Non-Financial MNE's, Ranked by Foreign Assets, 2016."

15. George Davis, "Boards Aren't as Global as Their Businesses," *Harvard Business Review*, October 28, 2014.

16. Nate Silver, "Education, Not Income, Predicted Who Would Vote for Trump," FiveThirtyEight.com, November 22, 2016.

17. Martin Rosenbaum, "Local Voting Figures Shed New Light on EU Referendum," BBC News, February 6, 2017.

18. Edna Bonacich, "A Theory of Ethnic Antagonism: The Split Labor Market," *American Sociological Review* 37, no. 5 (October 1972), pp. 547–59.

19. Gavin Wright, *Sharing the Prize: The Economics of the Civil Rights Revolution in the American South* (Cambridge, MA: Harvard University Press, 2013).

CHAPTER TWO: HUBS AND HEARTLANDS

1. For earlier versions of the argument in this chapter, see Michael Lind, "The Coming Realignment: Cities, Class, and Ideology After Social Conservatism," *Breakthrough Journal*, no. 4, Summer 2014; and Michael Lind, "Cities without Nations," *National Review*, September 26, 2016.

2. Saskia Sassen, *The Global City: New York, London, Tokyo* (Princeton: Princeton University Press, 2001); Saskia Sassen, "The Global City: Introducing a Concept," *Brown Journal of World Affairs* 11, no. 2 (Winter/ Spring, 2005).

3. Greg Rosalsky, "What the Future of Work Means for Cities," NPR, *Planet Money*, January 15, 2019; David Autor, "Work of the Past, Work of the Future," National Bureau of Economic Research Working Paper No. 25588, February 2019.

4. Richard Florida, "The High Inequality of U.S. Metro Areas Compared to Countries," CityLab.com, October 9, 2012.

5. William H. Frey, "The Suburbs: Not Just for White People Anymore," *New Republic*, November 24, 2014.

6. Richard Alba, "The Likely Persistence of a White Majority," *The American Prospect*, January 11, 2016; Stephen J. Trejo, "Who Remains Mexican? Selective Ethnic Attrition and the Intergenerational Progress of Mexican Americans," in David L. Leal and Stephen Trejo, eds. *Latinos and the Economy: Integration and Impact in Schools, Labor Markets, and Beyond* (Springer, 2010).

7. Michael Cembalest, "Pascal's Wager," *Eyes on the Market: Energy Outlook 2018*, Annual Energy Paper, J. P. Morgan, April 2018, p. 32.

8. William Jennings Bryan, "Cross of Gold" speech, July 8, 1896.

9. Adam Nossiter, "France Suspends Fuel Tax Increase That Spurred Violent Protests," *New York Times*, December 4, 2018.

10. Damien Cave, "It Was Supposed to Be Australia's Climate Change Election. What Happened?" *New York Times*, May 19, 2019.

11. David Autor, David Dorn, Gordon Hanson, and Kaveh Majlesi, "Importing Political Polarization? The Electoral Consequences of Rising Trade Exposure," National Bureau of Economic Research Working Paper No. 22637, September 2016, rev. December 2017.

12. Drew DeSilver, "Immigrants Don't Make Up a Majority of Workers in Any U.S. Industry," Pew Research Center, March 16, 2017.

13. Lynn Stuart Parramore, "America's New Servant Class," *AlterNet*, March 6, 2014.

14. Liz Sadler, "90 Percent of City Nannies Paid Off the Books," *New York Post*, March 10, 2010.

15. "Immigration and New York City: The Contributions of Foreign-Born Americans to New York's Renaissance, 1975–2013," This Americas Society/Council of the Americas, April 10, 2014.

16. Eric Kaufmann, *Whiteshift: Populism, Immigration, and the Future of White Majorities* (London: Allen Lane, 2018).

17. David Goodhart, *The Road to Somewhere: The Populist Revolt and the Future of Politics* (London: Hurst, 2017).

18. Quoctrung Bui and Claire Cain Miller, "The Typical American Lives Only 18 Miles from Mom," *New York Times*, December 23, 2015.

19. Haya Stier and Amit Kaplan, "Are Children a Joy or a Burden? Individual- and Macro-Level Characteristics and the Perception of Children," *European Journal of Population*, 2019.

20. D'Vera Cohn, Gretchen Livingston, and Wendy Wang, "Public Views on Staying at Home vs. Working," chapter 4 in "After Decades of Decline, a Rise in Stay-at-Home Mothers," Pew Research Center, 2014, p. 26.

21. Lisa Pickoff-White, Ryan Levi, "Are There Really More Dogs Than Children in S.F.?" KQED News, May 24, 2018.

22. Derek Thompson, "The Future of the City Is Childless," *Atlantic*, July 18, 2019.

23. Kenneth F. Scheve and Matthew J. Slaughter, "Labor Market Competition and Individual Preferences Over Immigration Policy," *Review of Economics and Statistics* 83, no. 1, February 2001, pp. 133–45.

24. Jens Hainmueller and Daniel J. Hopkins, "The Hidden American Immigration Consensus: A Conjoint Analysis of Attitudes Toward Immigrants," *American Journal of Political Science*, November 2014; Elias Naumann, Lukas F. Stoetzer, and Giuseppe Pietrantuono, "Attitudes Towards Highly Skilled and Low-Skilled Immigration in Europe: A Survey Experiment in 15 European Countries," *European Journal of Political Research* 57, no. 4, 2018, pp. 1009–30; Phillip Connor and Neil G. Ruiz, "Majority of U.S. Public Supports High-Skilled Immigration," Pew Research Center, January 22, 2019. According to Pew, even among those who want less overall immigration, half or more support more skilled immigration in the United States, Canada, the United Kingdom, Australia, Germany, France, Sweden, Austria, and Spain; the only exceptions are the Netherlands, Israel, and Italy.

CHAPTER THREE: WORLD WARS AND NEW DEALS

1. John Bates Clark, *The Control of Trusts* (New York: Macmillan, 1901), quoted in Michael Lind, *Land of Promise: An Economic History of the United States* (New York: HarperCollins, 2012), p. 213.

2. Joshua B. Freeman, *Behemoth: A History of the Factory and the Making of the Modern World* (New York: W. W. Norton, 2018), p. 93.

3. Quinn Slobodian, *Globalists: The End of Empire and the Birth of Neoliberalism* (Cambridge, MA: Harvard University Press, 2018).

4. Robert D. Atkinson and Michael Lind, *Big Is Beautiful: Debunking the Myth of Small Business* (Cambridge, MA: MIT Press, 2018).

5. Sheri Berman, *The Primacy of Politics* (Cambridge: Cambridge University Press, 2006).

6. Howard J. Wiarda, *Corporatism and Comparative Politics: The Other Great "Ism"* (Armonk, NY: M. E. Sharpe, 1996).

7. J. E. S. Hayward, "Solidarist Syndicalism: Durkheim and Duguit," *Sociological Review*, July 1960 (Part I) and December 1960 (Part II); M. J. Hawkins, "Durkheim on Occupational Corporations: An Exegesis and Interpretation," *Journal of the History of Ideas* 55, no. 3, July 1994, pp. 461–81.

8. Philippe C. Schmitter, "Still the Century of Corporatism?" *Review of Politics* 36, no. 1, January 1974, p. 103.

9. Paul Hirst, *The Pluralist Theory of the State: Selected Writings of G. D. H. Cole, J. N. Figgis, and H. J. Laski* (New York: Routledge, 2016); S. T. Glass, *The Responsible Society: The Ideas of Guild Socialism* (London: Longmans, 1966). For an attempt to revive English pluralism under the name of "associative democracy," see Paul Hirst and Veit Bader, eds., *Associative Democracy: The* Real *Third Way* (London: Frank Cass, 2001).

10. Bernard Semmel, *Imperialism and Social Reform: English Social-Imperial Thought, 1895–1914* (Cambridge, MA: Harvard University Press, 1960).

11. J. M. Winter, "Military Fitness and Civilian Health in Britain During the First World War," *Journal of Contemporary History* 15, no. 2, April 1980, p. 212.

12. Gunther Mai, *Das Ende des Kaiserreichs: Politik und Kriegsführung im Ersten Weltkrieg*, 3rd ed. (Munich: Deutscher Taschenbuch, 1997), p. 105, quoted in Herbert Obinger and Klaus Petersen, "Mass Warfare and the Welfare State—Causal Mechanisms and Effects," *British Journal of Political Science* 47, p. 218.

13. Larry G. Gerber, "Corporatism in Comparative Perspective: The Impact of the First World War on American and British Labor Relations," *Business History Review* 62, no. 1, Spring 1988, pp. 93–127, p. 99.

14. Marc Allen Eisner, *From Warfare State to Welfare State: World War I, Compensatory State Building, and the Limits of the Modern Order* (University Park: Pennsylvania State University Press, 2000), p. 309.

15. Robert Kuttner, *Can Democracy Survive Global Capitalism?* (New York: W. W. Norton, 2018), pp. 31–32.

16. Philippe C. Schmitter and Gerhard Lehmbruch, eds., *Trends Toward Corporatist Intermediation* (London: SAGE, 1979).

17. Jukka Pekkarinen, Matti Pohjola, and Bob Rowthorn, *Social Corporatism: A Superior Economic System?* (New York: Oxford University Press, 1992), p. 37.

18. Nelson Lichtenstein, *Labor's War at Home* (Cambridge: Cambridge University Press, 1982), p. 233.

19. Dwight D. Eisenhower, Letter to Edgar Newton Eisenhower, November 8, 1954.

20. Robert Griffith, "Dwight D. Eisenhower and the Corporate Commonwealth," *American Historical Review* 87, no. 1, February 1982, pp. 87–122.

21. Elizabeth Sanders, *Roots of Reform: Farmers, Workers, and the American State 1877–1917* (Chicago: University of Chicago Press, 1999).

22. Galbraith introduced the term in *American Capitalism: The Concept of Countervailing Power* (Boston: Houghton Mifflin, 1952).

23. William Forbath, "The Labor Movement Never Forgets?" *Law and Political Economy*, February 12, 2019.

24. John Chamberlain, *The American Stakes* (New York: Carrick & Evans, 1940), pp. 27–32.

25. Chamberlain, *The American Stakes*, p. 114.

CHAPTER FOUR: THE NEOLIBERAL
REVOLUTION FROM ABOVE

1. James Q. Wilson, *The Amateur Democrat: Club Politics in Three Cities* (Chicago: University of Chicago Press, 1962).

2. Theodore Lowi, "The Public Philosophy: Interest Group Liberalism," *American Political Science Review* 61, March 1967, pp. 5–24; and Theodore Lowi, *The End of Liberalism* (New York: Norton, 1969).

3. Nicholas Lemann, "Interest-Group Liberalism," *Washington Post*, October 21, 1986.

4. Alan Blinder, "Is Government Too Political?" *Foreign Affairs*, November/December 1997.

5. Quoted in Aaron Timms, "The Sameness of Cass Sunstein," *New Republic*, June 20, 2019; Cass Sunstein, *How Change Happens* (Cambridge, MA: MIT Press, 2019).

6. James S. Henry, "The Price of Offshore Revisited," Tax Justice Network, July 2012, cited in Robert Kuttner, *Can Democracy Survive Global Capitalism?* (New York: W. W. Norton, 2018), p. 230.

7. Jane Gravelle, "Tax Havens: International Tax Avoidance and Evasion," Congressional Research Service, January 2015, cited in Kuttner, *Can Democracy Survive Global Capitalism?*, p. 228.

8. Kuttner, *Can Democracy Survive Global Capitalism?*, p. 227.

9. Quoted in Daron Acemoglu and James A. Robinson, "How Do Populists Win?" Project Syndicate, May 31, 2019.

10. Stephen S. Roach, "Outsourcing, Protectionism, and the Global Labor Arbitrage," Morgan Stanley, November 11, 2003.

11. Richard Dobbs et al., "The World at Work: Jobs, Pay, and Skills for 3.5 Billion People," McKinsey Global Institute, January 2012.

12. Susan Lund, James Manyika, Jonathan Woetzel, Jacques Bughin, Mekala Krishnan, Jeongmin Seong, and Mac Muir, "Globalization in Transition: The Future of Trade and Value Chains," McKinsey Global Institute, January 2019. Source of statistics: "Country Comparison: GDP Per Capita (PPP)," *The World Factbook*, United States Central Intelligence Agency (CIA), https://www.cia.gov/library/publications/the-world-factbook/rankorder/2004rank.html, accessed September 24, 2019.

13. Michael Spence, "The Restructuring of the World," Project Syndicate, September 27, 2018.

14. Kevin B. Barefoot and Raymond J. Mataloni Jr., "U.S. Multinational Companies: Operations in the United States and Abroad Preliminary Results from the 2009 Benchmark Survey," *Survey of Current Business*, November 2011; David Wessel, "U.S. Firms Keen to Add Foreign Jobs," *Wall Street Journal*, November 22, 2011.

15. Delia D. Aguilar, "Introduction," in Delia D. Aguilar and Anne E. Lacsamana, eds., *Women and Globalization* (Amherst, NY: Humanity Books, 2004), pp. 16–17, cited in Hester Eisenstein, *Feminism*

Seduced: How Global Elites Use Women's Labor and Ideas to Exploit the World (Boulder, CO: Paradigm, 2009), p. 17.

16. David H. Autor, David Dorn, and Gordon H. Hanson, "The China Shock: Learning from Labor-Market Adjustment to Large Changes in Trade," *Annual Review of Economics* 8, October 2016, pp. 205–40; Daron Acemoglu, David Autor, David Dorn, Gordon H. Hanson, and Brendan Price, "Import Competition and the Great U.S. Employment Sag of the 2000s," National Bureau of Economic Research Working Paper No. 20395, August 2014.

17. Michael W. L. Elsby, Bart Hobijn, and Aysegul Sahin, "The Decline of the U.S. Labor Share," *Brookings Papers on Economic Activity*, Fall 2013.

18. Konstantin Kakaes, "The All-American iPhone," *MIT Technology Review*, June 9, 2016.

19. Intan Suwandi, R. Jamil Jonna, and John Bellamy Foster, "Global Commodity Chains and the New Imperialism," *Monthly Review*, March 2019.

20. Chance Miller, "Phone X Said to Cost Apple $357 to Make, Gross Margin Higher than iPhone 8," 9to5mac.com, November 6, 2017.

21. United States Senate Homeland Security and Government Affairs Permanent Subcommittee on Investigations, "Subcommittee to Examine Offshore Profit Shifting and Tax Avoidance by Apple Inc.," March 20, 2013.

22. Nick Hopkins and Simon Bowers, "Apple Secretly Moved Parts of Empire to Jersey After Row Over Tax Affairs," *Guardian*, November 6, 2017.

23. Adam Smith, *An Inquiry into the Nature and Causes of the Wealth Of Nations*, Book VI, Chapter II, "Of the Sources of the General or Public Revenue of the Society," Part II, "Of Taxes," Article II, "Taxes Upon Profit, or Upon the Revenue Arising from Stock," Project Gutenberg ebook of *An Inquiry into the Nature and Causes of the Wealth of Nations*, ebook #3300, accessed October 3, 2019, https://www.gutenberg.org/files/3300/3300-h/3300-h.htm#chap11.

24. Smith, *An Inquiry*, Book I, Chapter IX, "On the Profits of Stock."

25. Peter Mair, *Ruling the Void: The Hollowing of Western Democracy* (London: Verso, 2013), p. 1.

26. Wolfgang Streeck and Philippe C. Schmitter, "From National Corporatism to Transnational Pluralism: Organized Interests in the Single European Market," *Politics and Society*, June 1, 1991.

27. David Skelton, "Government of the Technocrats, by the Technocrats, for the Technocrats," *New Statesman*, November 16, 2011; James Mackenzie, Diana Khyriakidou, "A Tale of Two Technocrats: Paths Diverge for Greece and Italy," Reuters, February 3, 2012.

28. David A. Kaplan, *The Most Dangerous Branch: Inside the Supreme Court's Assault on the Constitution* (New York: Crown, 2018).

29. Ran Hirschl, *Towards Juristocracy: The Origins and Consequences of the New Constitutionalism* (Cambridge, MA: Harvard University Press, 2004), pp. 1, 15, 214.

30. Robert D. Putnam, *Bowling Alone: The Collapse and Revival of American Community* (New York: Simon & Schuster, 2000).

31. Theda Skocpol, Rachael V. Cobb, and Casey Andrew Klofstad, "Disconnection and Reorganization: The Transformation of Civic Life in Late-Twentieth-Century America," *Studies in American Political Development* 19, Fall 2005, pp. 137–56. See also Theda Skocpol, *Diminished Democracy: From Membership to Management in American Civic Life* (Norman: University of Oklahoma Press, 2003).

32. Ben Stein, "In Class Warfare, Guess Which Class Is Winning," *New York Times*, November 26, 2006.

CHAPTER FIVE: THE POPULIST COUNTERREVOLUTION FROM BELOW

1. Matthew Goodwin, "Why National Populism Is Here to Stay," *New Statesman*, October 3, 2018.

2. Lee Drutman, "What Donald Trump Gets About the Electorate," *Vox*, August 18, 2015.

3. Matt Karp, "51 Percent Losers," *Jacobin*, November 14, 2018.

4. Thomas B. Edsall, "We Aren't Seeing White Support for Trump for What It Is," *New York Times*, August 28, 2019.

5. "Germany's Green Party Finds a Haven in Heidelberg," DW.com, July 24, 2017.

6. Vernon Briggs, "Illegal Immigration and the Dilemma of American Unions," History News Network, March 7, 2011.

7. U.S. Commission on Immigration Reform, "Legal Immigration: Setting Priorities" (Washington, DC: U.S. Commission on Immigration Reform, 1996); U.S. Commission on Immigration Reform, "Becoming an American: Immigration and Immigrant Policy" (Washington, D.C.: U.S. Commission on Immigration Reform, 1997).

8. Quoted in Rhonda Fanning, "What Barbara Jordan & Current GOP Rhetoric Have in Common," Texas Standard, February 16, 2016.

9. Erik Ruark, "Misuse of Barbara Jordan's Legacy on Immigration is Wrong, No Matter Who Does It," NumbersUSA, January 17, 2019.

10. Vernon M. Briggs Jr. *Immigration and American Unionism* (ILR Press, 2001).

11. Phillip Connor and Jens Manuel Krogstad, "Immigration Might Be Out of Favour but 'Outmigration' Is Even More Unpopular," World Economic Forum, December 12, 2018.

12. Monthly Harvard CAPS / Harris Poll June 2018, cited in Jeff Faux, "Trump Is Laying a Trap for Democrats on Immigration," *The Nation*, April 2, 2019.

13. Lee Jones, "Labour's Brexit Capitulation Is the End of Corbynism," *Brexit Blog*, London School of Economics, July 17, 2019.

14. The Editors, "Against Trump," *National Review*, January 22, 2016.

15. David Marquand, "Pluralism v Populism," *Prospect*, June 20, 1999.

16. Robert Nisbet, *The Quest for Community* (New York: Oxford University Press, 1973 [1953]), p. 270.

17. Carlos de la Torre and Cynthia J. Arnson, *Latin American Populism in the Twenty-First Century* (Washington, DC: Woodrow Wilson Center Press, 2013).

18. T. Harry Williams, *Huey Long* (New York: Knopf, 1970).

19. Carol O'Keefe Wilson, *In the Governor's Shadow: The True Story of Ma and Pa Ferguson* (Denton: University of North Texas Press, 2014).

CHAPTER SIX: RUSSIAN PUPPETS AND NAZIS

1. The term "Brown Scare" was coined by Leo P. Ribuffo, in *The Old Christian Right: The Protestant Far Right from the Great Depression to the Cold War* (Philadelphia: Temple University Press, 1983). See also Gary Alan Fine and Terence McDonnell, "Erasing the Brown Scare: Referential Afterlife and the Power of Memory Templates," *Social Problems* 54, no. 2 (May 2007), pp. 170–87.

2. David Marcus, "Antifa Is Mostly Made Up of Privileged White Dudes," *The Federalist*, July 1, 2019.

3. Carol Matlack and Robert Williams, "France to Probe Possible Russian Influence on Yellow Vest Riots," Bloomberg, December 7, 2018; "Exposed: Russian Twitter Bots Tried to Swing General Election for Jeremy Corbyn," *Sunday Times*, April 29, 2018.

4. Matt Taibbi, "As the Mueller Probe Ends, New Russiagate Myths Begin," *Rolling Stone*, March 25, 2019.

5. Jeffrey M. Jones, "More in U.S. Favor Diplomacy Over Sanctions for Russia," Gallup, August 20, 2018.

6. Aaron Mate, "New Studies Show Pundits Are Wrong About Russian Social-Media Involvement in US Politics," *The Nation*, December 28, 2018.

7. Scott Shane, "These Are the Ads Russia Bought on Facebook in 2016," *New York Times*, November 1, 2017; Scott Shane and Sheera Frenkel, "Russian 2016 Influence Operation Targeted African-Americans on Social Media," *New York Times*, December 17, 2018.

8. Jason Guerrasio, "We Asked Michael Moore About the Gun-Violence Epidemic, His New Movie, and Why Donald Trump Will Get the Republican Nomination," *Business Insider*, December 23, 2015.

9. Michael Moore, "5 Reasons Why Trump Will Win," michaelmoore.com.

10. Alex Seitz-Wald and Benjy Sarlin, "Why Democrats Fear Donald Trump," NBC News, February 26, 2016.

11. Amanda Sakuma, "Trump Did Better With Blacks, Hispanics Than Romney in '12: Exit Polls," NBC News, November 9, 2016.

12. "Populism Past and Present," hammer.ucla.edu/programs-events/2016/05/populism-past-and-present.

13. Alan I. Abramowitz, "Did Russian Interference Affect the 2016 Election Results?" Sabato's Crystal Ball, August 8, 2019.

14. Ben Riley-Smith, "Hillary Clinton Questions Whether Cambridge Analytica Helped the Russians Meddle in 2016 Election," *Daily Telegraph*, March 20, 2018.

15. Albright, *Fascism: A Warning* (New York: Harper, 2018).

16. Jason Stanley, *How Fascism Works: The Politics of Us and Them* (New York: Random House, 2018).

17. Zack Beauchamp, "A Leading Holocaust Historian Just Seriously Compared the US to Nazi Germany," *Vox*, October 5, 2018).

18. Christopher R. Browning, "The Suffocation of Democracy," *New York Review of Books*, October 25, 2018.

19. Carly Sitrin, "Read: President Trump's Remarks Condemning Violence 'On Many Sides' in Charlottesville," *Vox*, August 12, 2017.

20. "Statement by President Trump," August 14, 2017, whitehouse.gov.

21. "Full Transcript and Video: Trump's News Conference in New York," August 15, 2017.

22. Joe Heim, "Recounting a Day of Rage, Hate, Violence and Death," *Washington Post*, August 14, 2017; Matt Pearce, "Who Was Responsible for the Violence in Charlottesville? Here's What Witnesses Say," *Los Angeles Times*, August 15, 2017.

23. Chris Kahn, "A Majority of Americans Want to Preserve Confederate Monuments: Reuters/Ipsos Poll," Reuters, August 21, 2017; "Trump's Domestic Crisis: Charlottesville and White Nationalists," August 16, 2017, yougov.com.

24. "NPR/PBS NewsHour/Marist Poll Results on Charlotteseville," August 17, 2017, maristpoll.marist.edu.

25. Volker Ullrlich, *Hitler: Ascent 1889–1939* (New York: Vintage, 2017), p. 117.

26. Martin Roiser and Carla Willig, "The Strange Death of the Authoritarian Personality: 50 Years of Psychological and Political Debate," *History of the Human Sciences* 15, no. 4, p. 74; Theodor Adorno, Else Frenkel-Brenswik, Daniel J. Levinson, R. Nevitt Sanford, *The Authoritarian Personality* (New York: Harper & Row, 1950).

27. Bob Altemeyer, *The Authoritarian Specter* (Cambridge, MA: Harvard University Press, 1996), p. 5.

28. Right Wing Authoritarian Test, openpsychometrics.org, accessed February 28, 2019.

29. Jesse Singal, "How Social Science Might Be Misunderstanding Conservatives," *New York*, July 15, 2018.

30. Theodor W. Adorno and Jamie Owen Daniel, "On Jazz," *Discourse* 12, no. 1, A Special Issue on Music (Fall–Winter 1989–90), pp. 45–69.

31. Jesse Singal, "How Social Science."

32. Daniel Bell, ed., *The New American Right* (New York: Criterion Books, 1955); Daniel Bell, ed., *Radical Right: The New American Right Expanded and Updated* (Garden City, NY: Doubleday and Company, Inc., 1963).

33. Richard Hofstadter, "The Pseudo-Conservative Revolt," *American Scholar* 24 (Winter 1954–1955), pp. 11–17.

34. Nils Gilman, "Revisiting Hofstadter's Populism," *The American Interest* 14, no. 1, May 2018.

35. On agrarian populism, see Lawrence Goodwyn, *The Populist Moment: A Short History of the Agrarian Revolt in America* (Oxford University Press, 1978); Michael Kazin, *The Populist Persuasion: An American History* (Basic Books, 1995); Charles Postel, *The Populist Vision* (Oxford University Press, 2007); Anton Jäger, "The Myth of Populism," *Jacobin* (January 3, 2018).

36. Jon Wiener, "America, Through a Glass Darkly," *The Nation*, October 5, 2006.

37. C. Vann Woodward, "The Populist Heritage and the Intellectual," *American Scholar* 29, no. 1 (Winter 1959–60), pp. 55–72.

38. Michael Paul Rogin, *The Intellectuals and McCarthy: The Radical Specter* (Cambridge, MA: MIT Press, 1967).

39. Richard Hofstadter, "The Paranoid Style in American Politics," *Harper's*, November 1964.

40. Elizabeth Tandy Shermer, *Sunbelt Capitalism: Phoenix and the Transformation of American Politics* (University of Pennsylvania Press, 2013); Matthew D. Lassiter, *The Silent Majority: Suburban Politics in the Sunbelt*

South (Princeton, NJ: Princeton University Press, 2006). See Kim Phillips-Fein, "Conservatism: A State of the Field," *Journal of American History* 98, no. 3, December 2011, pp. 723–43.

41. John Levi Martin, "The Authoritarian Personality, 50 Years Later. What Lessons Are there for Political Psychology?" *Political Psychology* 22, p. 1 (2001).

42. Henry Giroux, "Trump's Fascist Efforts to Demolish Democracy," *The Conversation*, November 25, 2018.

43. Matthew MacWilliams, "The One Weird Trait That Predicts Whether You're a Trump Supporter," *Politico*, January 17, 2016.

44. Sean Illing, "Why Trump's Populist Appeal Is About Culture, Not the Economy," *Vox*, March 27, 2017.

45. Leo P. Ribuffo, "Donald Trump and 'the Paranoid Style' in American Politics," H-Diplo/ISSF, June 13, 2017.

46. Norman Pollack, "Hofstadter on Populism: A Critique of 'The Age of Reform,'" *Journal of Southern History* 26, no. 4 (November 1960), pp 495–96.

47. Christopher Lasch, *The Culture of Narcissism: American Life in an Age of Diminishing Expectations* (New York: W. W. Norton, 1978); Lasch, "Life in the Therapeutic State," *New York Review of Books*, June 12, 1980.

48. Katie Reilly, "Read Hillary Clinton's 'Basket of Deplorables' Remarks About Donald Trump Supporters," *Time*, September 10, 2016.

49. G. Wilkinson, "Political Dissent and 'Sluggish Schizophrenia' in the Soviet Union," *British Medical Journal*, September 1986, pp. 641–42.

50. Louis Hartz, *The Liberal Tradition in America: An Interpretation of American Political Thought Since the Revolution* (Harcourt Brace, 1955).

CHAPTER SEVEN: THE WORKERLESS PARADISE

1. Charlie Duxbury, "Danish Social Democrats Win National Election," *Politico*, June 5, 2019.

2. Ralph Miliband, *Socialism for a Sceptical Age* (London: Verso, 1994), p. 16.

3. Bureau of Labor Statistics, United States Department of Labor, "Employment Projections," accessed December 16, 2018.

4. James K. Galbraith, *Inequality and Instability: A Study of the World Economy Just Before the Great Crisis* (New York: Oxford University Press, 2012).

5. T. Kristal, "Good Times, Bad Times: Postwar Labor's Share of Income in Capitalist Democracies," *American Sociological Review* 75, no. 5, October 2010, pp. 729–63, cited in Andrew Sayer, *Why We Can't Afford the Rich* (Chicago: Policy Press, 2016), pp. 187–88.

6. J. Peters, "The Rise of Finance and the Decline of Organized Labor in the Advanced Capitalist Countries," *New Political Economy* 16, no. 1, p. 93, cited in Sayer, *Why We Can't Afford the Rich*, pp. 187–88.

7. Chang-Tai Hsieh and Enrico Moretti, "Why Do Cities Matter? Local Growth and Aggregate Growth," Chicago Unbound: Kreisman Working Paper Series in Housing Law and Policy, 2015.

8. Shirin Ghaffary, "Many in Silicon Valley Support Universal Basic Income. Now the California Democratic Party Does, Too," *Vox*, March 8, 2018; Candice Norwood, "Silicon Valley Is Helping Cities Test a Radical Anti-Poverty Idea," *Governing*, July 16, 2018.

9. Barry C. Lynn, *Cornered: The New Monopoly and the Economics of Destruction* (New York: John Wiley & Sons, 2010); Lina M. Khan, "Amazon's Antitrust Paradox," *Yale Law Journal* 126, no. 3, January 2017; Matt Stoller, *Goliath: The 100-Year War Between Monopoly Power and Democracy* (New York: Simon & Schuster, 2019).

10. Robert D. Atkinson and Michael Lind, *Big Is Beautiful: Debunking the Myth of Small Business* (Cambridge, MA: MIT Press, 2018), p. 65.

11. Atkinson and Lind, *Big Is Beautiful*, p. 65.

12. Charles Lamb, *A Dissertation Upon Roast Pig: One of the Essays of Elia, with a Note on Lamb's Literary Motive* (Palala Press, 2016).

13. Milton Friedman, *Capitalism and Freedom* (Chicago: University of Chicago Press, 1962); Charles Murray, *In Our Hands: A Plan to Replace the Welfare State* (Washington, DC: AEI Press, 2016).

14. Daniel McCarthy, "A New Conservative Agenda: A Governing Philosophy for the Twenty-First Century," *First Things*, March 2019.

CHAPTER EIGHT: COUNTERVAILING POWER

1. David Marquand, "Pluralism v Populism," *Prospect*, June 20, 1999.

2. Kate Andrias, "The New Labor Law," *Yale Law Journal* 126, no. 1, October 2016; Mark Barenberg, "Widening the Scope of Labor Organizing: Legal Reforms to Facilitate Multi-Employer Organizing, Bargaining, and Striking," Roosevelt Institute, October 7, 2015; David Madland, "The Future of Worker Voice and Power," Center for American Progress, October 11, 2016.

3. Robert A. Dahl, *After the Revolution? Authority in a Good Society*, rev. ed. (New Haven, CT: Yale University Press, 1990 [1970]), p. 132.

4. Mia Sato, "What the Gov: What Does It Mean to Have Six Democratic Socialists on the Chicago City Council?" Better Government Association, July 2, 2019.

5. Ganesh Sitaraman and Anne L. Alstott, *The Public Option: How to Expand Freedom, Increase Opportunity, and Promote Equality* (Cambridge, MA: Harvard University Press, 2019).

6. Kirkpatrick Sale, *Human Scale Revisited: A New Look at the Classic Case for a Decentralist Future* (White River Junction, VT: Chelsea Green, 2017), pp. 145–46.

7. John Gray, *Two Faces of Liberalism* (New York: The New Press, 2000).

8. Tara Isabella Burton, "Corporations Are Replacing Churches as America's Conscience," *Vox*, August 18, 2017.

9. Benjamin Fearnow, "Number of Witches Rises Dramatically Across U.S. as Millennials Reject Christianity," *Newsweek*, November 18, 2018; Pew forum on religion and public life, "U.S. Religious Landscape Survey: Religious Beliefs and Practices: Diverse and Politically Relevant" (Washington, DC: Pew Research Center, 2008).

CHAPTER NINE: MAKING THE WORLD SAFE FOR DEMOCRATIC PLURALISM

1. Dani Rodrik, "The Inescapable Trilemma of the World Economy," author's blog, June 17, 2000. See Dani Rodrik, "How Far Will

International Economic Integration Go?" *Journal of Economic Perspectives* 14, no. 1, 2000, pp. 177–86.

2. Robert D. Atkinson and Michael Lind, "National Developmentalism: From Forgotten Tradition to New Consensus," *American Affairs* 3, no. 2 (Summer 2019).

3. Chalmers Johnson, *MITI and the Japanese Miracle: The Growth of Industrial Policy, 1925–1975* (Stanford, CA: Stanford University Press, 1982); Alice Amsden, *Asia's Next Giant: South Korea and Late Industrialization* (New York: Oxford University Press, 1989); Meredith Woo-Cumings, *The Developmental State* (Ithaca, NY: Cornell University Press, 1999).

4. Erik Reinert, *How Rich Countries Got Rich and Why Poor Countries Stay Poor* (London: Constable, 2007); Ha-Joon Chang, *Kicking Away the Ladder: Development Strategy in Historical Perspective* (London: Anthem Press, 2002); Michael Hudson, *America's Protectionist Takeoff, 1815–1914* (Dresden, Germany: ISLET, 2010).

5. Oxford Economics, "Understanding the US-China Trade Relationship," paper prepared for the US-China Business Council, January 2017.

6. Vincent Navarro, "The Worldwide Class Struggle," in Michael D. Yates, ed., *More Unequal: Aspects of Class in the United States* (New York: Monthly Review Press, 2007), p. 23.

7. Dani Rodrik, *Straight Talk on Trade: Ideas for a Sane World Economy* (Princeton, NJ: Princeton University Press, 2018), p. 92.

8. Jonas Pontusson, David Rueda, and Christopher R. Way, "Comparative Political Economy of Wage Distribution: The Role of Partisanship and Labour Market Institutions," *British Journal of Political Science* 32, no. 2, 2002, pp. 281–308; Bruce Western and Jake Rosenfeld, "Unions, Norms, and the Rise in U.S. Wage Inequality," *American Sociological Review* 76, no. 4, 2001, pp. 513–37; David Card, Thomas Lemieux, and W. Craig Riddell, "Unions and Wage Inequality," *Journal of Labor Research* 25, no. 4, 2004, pp. 519–59.

9. United States Department of Labor, Bureau of Labor Statistics, "Union Members Summary," Economic News Release, January 18, 2019.

10. Niall McCarthy, "Which Countries Have the Highest Levels of Labor Union Membership? [Infographic]," *Forbes*, June 20, 2017.

11. Western and Rosenfeld, "Unions, Norms, and the Rise in U.S. Wage Inequality."

12. Robert Kuttner, *Can Democracy Survive Global Capitalism?* (New York: W. W. Norton, 2018), p. 132.

13. Micheline Maynard, "The UAW Is Losing Its Grip on Auto Industry Labor," *Forbes*, February 20, 2014; David Welch and Nacha Cattan, "How Mexico's Unions Sell Out Autoworkers," Bloomberg, May 5, 2017.

14. See, for example, Sapna Jain, "Can We Keep Meatpacking Companies Accountable for Hiring Undocumented Immigrants?" *Emory Corporate Governance and Accountability Review* 3, 2016, pp. 157–69.

15. Kate Bronfenbrenner, *Uneasy Terrain* (Ithaca, NY: ILF Collection, 2000).

16. Milton Friedman, "What Is America," lecture at Stanford University, quoted in Judith Gans, Elaine M. Replogle, and Daniel J. Tichenor, eds., *Debates on U.S. Immigration* (Thousand Oaks, CA: SAGE, 2012), p. 227.

17. Paul Krugman, "North of the Border," *New York Times*, March 27, 2006.

18. United Press International, "Bloomberg: Illegal Immigrants Help Golfers," UPI.com, April 1, 2006.

19. Dave Seminara, "Bush 43's Bankrupt 'Let Them Pick Cotton' Immigration Policy," *The Hill*, February 19, 2019.

20. Ken Webster Jr., "Beto Tells Black Guy: We Need Illegal Immigrants for Cotton Gin," kprcradio.iheart.com, September 20, 2018.

21. Natalie Kitroeff, "Immigrants Flooded California Construction. Worker Pay Sank. Here's Why," *Los Angeles Times*, April 22, 2017; Sara Murray, "On the Killing Floor, Clues to the Impact of Immigration on Jobs," *Wall Street Journal*, August 21, 2013; Philip Martin, *Importing Poverty? Immigration and the Changing Face of Rural America* (New Haven, CT: Yale University Press, 2009).

22. Robert Shapiro, "Race, Ethnicity, and the Job Market," *Journal of Democracy*, no. 53, Summer 2019.

23. Patricia Cohen, "Is Immigration at Its Limit? Not for Employers," *New York Times*, August 22, 2019.

24. Matthew Yglesias, "DREAM On: America Needs Much Bigger, Bolder Immigration Reform—for Low-Skilled Workers, Not Just Supergeniuses—to Boost the Economy," *Slate*, June 20, 2012.

25. "The Impact of Illegal Immigration on the Wages and Employment Opportunities of Black Workers: A Briefing Before the United States Commission on Civil Rights" (Washington, DC: U.S. Commission on Civil Rights, August 2010).

26. National Academies of Sciences, Engineering, and Medicine, *The Economic and Fiscal Consequences of Immigration* (Washington, DC: National Academies Press, 2017).

27. Mark Zuckerberg, "Immigrants Are the Key to a Knowledge Economy," *Washington Post*, April 10, 2013.

28. Michael Lind, "Reich Is Wrong: Immigration Won't Solve Entitlement Mess," *Salon*, April 13, 2010.

29. Steven A. Camarota and Karen Zeigler, "Projecting the Impact of Immigration on the U.S. Population: A Look at Size and Age Structure through 2060," Center for Immigration Studies, February 4, 2019.

30. Steven A. Camarota and Karen Zeigler, "Projecting the Impact of Immigration on the U.S. Population," Center for Immigration Studies, February 2019.

31. Michael Lind, "Reich Is Wrong."

32. Michael Lind, "The Two-Year Solution," *New York Times*, June 1, 2007.

33. John B. Judis, *The Nationalist Revival: Trade, Immigration, and the Revolt Against Globalization* (New York: Columbia Global Reports, 2018), p. 146.

Index